The Complete Book of Science Grades 1-2

Table of Contents

D0127662

Section 1
Human Body

Name _____

How Did You Do That?

You use many parts of your body to do even the simplest activities.

Read each activity, and write the body parts you would use to do that activity.

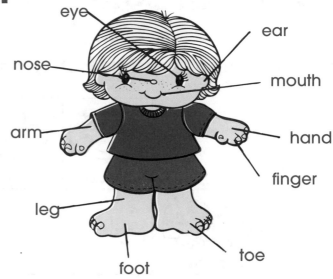

eye
ear
nose
mouth
arm
hand
finger
leg
toe
foot

Activities:

1. Read a book.

2. Talk to your friend on the phone.

3. Put on your hat.

4. Blow out the candles on a cake.

5. Eat an ice-cream cone.

6. Ride a bike to school.

Name _____

Move That Body

Read each task on the chart. Color the spaces on the chart which show the parts of the body that would be used for the task.

Tasks	head	arms	hands	legs	feet
wash dishes					
pull weeds					
play soccer					
play on a slide					
use a skateboard					
$2 + 2 = 4$ do homework					
play catch					

Name _____

Body Works

Read the clues. Write the words in the puzzle.

Across:
2. You use these to breathe.
4. You need to do this when you're tired.
5. This breaks down food.
7. This tells your body what to do.
9. This is a gas you breathe.
10. It pumps blood.

Down:
2. It carries oxygen to your body.
3. Tiny living things that can make you sick.
6. This helps you when you are sick.
8. These support and shape your body.

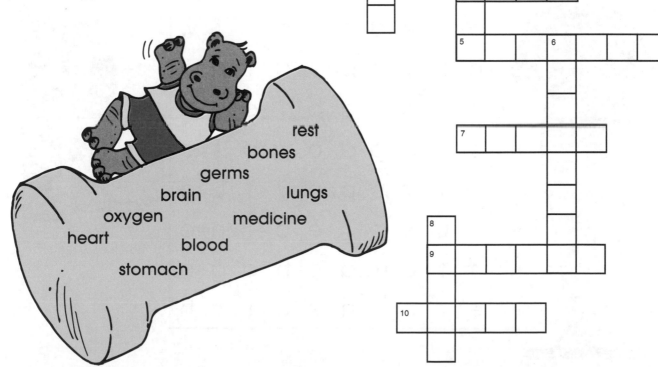

rest
bones
germs
brain   lungs
oxygen   medicine
heart   blood
stomach

Name _____

Body Language

Circle the words that are part of your body.

Word Bank				
head	arm	foot	brain	skeleton
bone	skin	blood	heart	windpipe
lungs	eye	muscle	teeth	stomach

```
a t e e t h o y i u
n e s q h e a d r t
l u k w f a r u t s
l d e i o r m e s d
s k l n o t z y k e
o m e d t s b e i w
h e t p b r a i n i
t c o i q b l o o d
s a n p d o w b l s
w i m e p n i t u a
m u s c l e c l n e
s t o m a c h a g n
e r o y n k o r s h
```

Body Buddies

Arrange the numbers to print a word that is part of your body.
Then, color each part.

_____ brown

1. a r n i b
   3 2 5 4 1

_____ green

2. n e k e
   2 3 1 4

_____ yellow

3. m o t c a h s
   4 3 2 6 5 7 1

_____ red

4. t a e h r
   5 3 2 1 4

_____ blue

5. s u l g n
   5 2 1 4 3

_____ orange

6. s e b o n
   5 4 1 2 3

_____ pink

7. d p i n w i e p
   4 5 6 3 1 2 8 7

_____ purple

8. i k y e n d s
   2 1 6 5 4 3 7

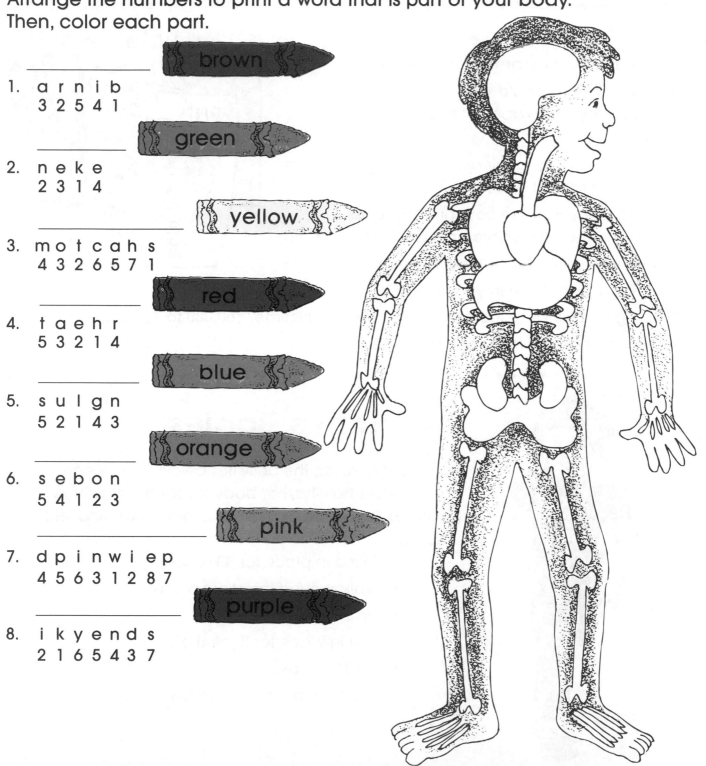

Fun Facts About You!

Each day, ask your child one of the "fun facts" below.

- How many muscles are in our bodies? (656)
- How many times could your blood vessels go around the world? (about 4 times around the equator)
- How many gallons of air do we breathe every day? (about 5,000)
- How old are you when your brain reaches its full weight of about three pounds? (16 years old)
- How long is your small intestine? (22 feet)
- How many bones are in your skull? (22)
- How many pounds of food will you eat in your lifetime? (60,000 to 100,000)
- How many bones are in our bodies? (206)

Our Active Bodies

Have your child do the activities below. In between each, discuss how his/her body responds (heartbeat increases, breathing heavier and faster, sweating, etc.).

- Stand in place for 30 seconds.
- Walk around the room 6 times.
- Do 25 jumping jacks.
- Jog in place for 3 minutes.
- Do 15 sit-ups.
- March in place for 2 minutes.

My Body Homework

Give your child the chart below and discuss it with him/her. Explain that in order to keep his/her body working and looking its best, he/she should start good health habits now and continue them as he/she grows older. He/she should use this checklist to keep "on track" with good health habits for the next week. Tell your child that he/she should keep his/her chart on the bathroom mirror or on a night stand in his/her bedroom as a reminder.

Name	Sun.	Mon.	Tues.	Wed.	Thurs.	Fri.	Sat.
I slept at least 8 hours.							
I ate a healthful breakfast.							
I brushed my teeth this morning.							
I ate a healthful lunch.							
I washed my hands after using the bathroom.							
I exercised at least 30 minutes today.							
I drank at least 6 glasses of water.							
I stood and sat up straight.							
I ate a healthful dinner.							
I took a bath or shower.							
I brushed my teeth this evening.							

This page intentionally left blank.

Outfitted for Health

Read the phrases in the Word Bank. Write only the **good** health habits on the lines.

Word Bank	Take a bath. Drink water. Sit all day. Exercise.	Eat lots of sweets. Get plenty of sleep. Never wash your hands. Eat healthful foods.	Stay up all night. Keep cuts clean. Brush your teeth.

1. _____

2. _____

3. _____

4. _____

5. _____

6. _____

7. _____

Mighty Muscles

EXPERIMENT Make a Muscle

The body has over 600 muscles, each with its own special job of helping the body move. Ask your child which one of his/her muscles he/she thinks is the strongest. (It's the heart.) Then, let your child try the experiment below to see how his/her muscles work.

You will need:

two 9" x 2" pieces of tagboard
one brass fastener
one 9" and one 12" piece of string
tape

Directions:

Help your child lay the tagboard pieces overlapping end-to-end and connect them with the fastener. (See diagram.) Then, tape the 9" piece of string centered along one side of the connected pieces, and the 12" string loosely centered along the other side of the connected pieces. Explain to your child that this is what a relaxed muscle is like, similar to when his/her arm is hanging at his/her side. Place the "arm" on a table, and have your child pull the short string to "flex" the "muscle." To straighten the "arm" again, have your child pull the longer string.

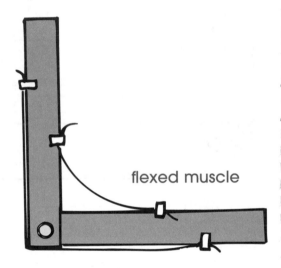

flexed muscle

relaxed muscle

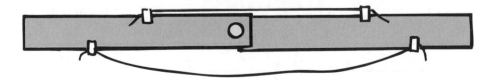

Find Your Strong Side

EXPERIMENT

You will need:

two 8 ½" x 12" sheets of construction paper
pencils
scissors
tape

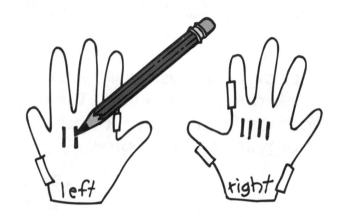

Directions:

Explain to your child that the brain has two sides that tell the body what to do. One side may be stronger than the other. The left side of the brain controls the right side of the body, and the right side of the brain controls the left side. Let your child try the experiment below to find out which side of his/her brain he/she uses the most.

Have your child trace both hands on the construction paper and label them **left** and **right**. Then, have your child cut out the hands and tape them to a flat surface. Read the following instructions aloud.

Ask your child to observe which side he/she uses and to record it on the cut-out hands using a tally mark as shown in the illustration.

- Clasp your hands together. Which hand is on top?
- Take three steps. Which foot did you start with?
- Try to do the splits. Which leg is in front?
- Pick up your pencil to write. Which hand did you use?
- Wink one eye. Which eye did you use?
- Fold your arms. Which arm is on top?

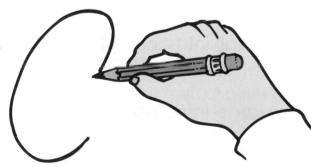

Add the total number of times each side was used.
Ask your child if one side of his/her brain is stronger than the other. Ask which one, but don't let your child forget that the **left** side of the brain controls the **right** side of the body, and the **right** side of the brain controls the **left** side of the body!

Eating Good Food

The food you eat takes a long trip through your digestive system. Foods are broken down during the journey. The nutrients from the food give your body energy to work and grow.

Color the parts of your digestive system.

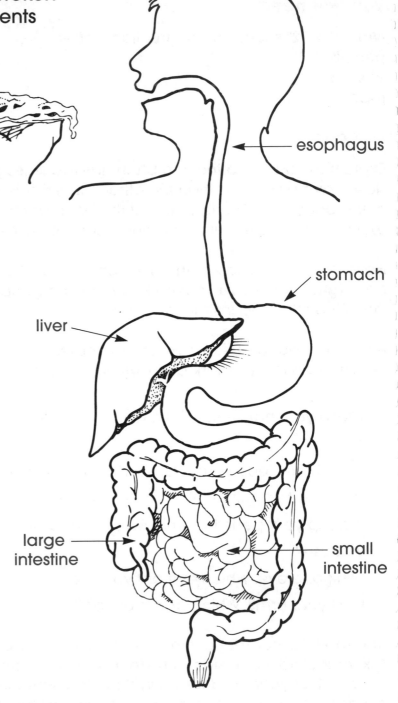

esophagus - yellow

stomach - **red**

small intestine - **blue**

large intestine - green

liver - **brown**

Digest This!

Ask your child if he/she has ever wondered what happens to his/her food after he/she takes a bite of it. Explain that first the teeth cut and grind it, then the stomach works to crush it down into very small pieces. Let your child try the experiments below to learn more about his/her digestive system.

EXPERIMENT Chomp! Chomp!

Have your child slowly bite saltine crackers in half with his/her front teeth, then continue chewing as the food is made smaller and passed toward the back of the mouth. Discuss how the texture has changed.

EXPERIMENT Yummy in My Tummy!

You will need:
3 clear cups
2 tablespoons of honey
peanut butter
dry milk and spoons

Directions:

Explain to your child that the function of the stomach is digesting foods into a liquid mixture. Ask your child to predict which of the three foods used would mix and digest the easiest. Let your child find out by adding one of the ingredients to each cup and filling it $\frac{3}{4}$ full with water. Have your child stir each cup every 2-3 hours. Ask him/her questions, such as "Which dissolves most easily?" "Which would digest most easily?" and "Can you think of any other foods that may be easy/hard to digest?"

Bones Give You Shape

Word Bank		
skull	ribs	foot
hand	knee	hips

Bones give your body shape. They help you stand up tall. You cannot see your bones. But you can feel many of your bones under your skin.

Draw a line from each bone to the part of the body where it is found. Use the Word Bank to help you write the name of each bone.

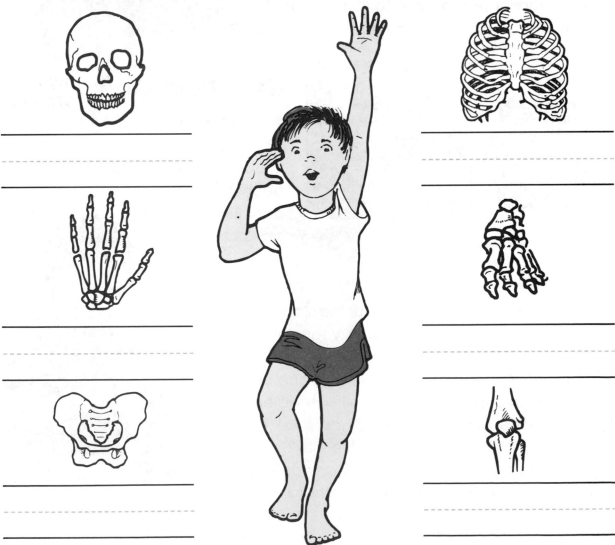

Name _____

Crossbones

Across:

3. They protect your heart and lungs.
6. All of your bones.
7. It connects your leg and foot.

Down:

1. Found on the end of your hands.
2. Found on the end of your feet.
4. Your spine.
5. It makes your leg bend.
6. This protects your brain.

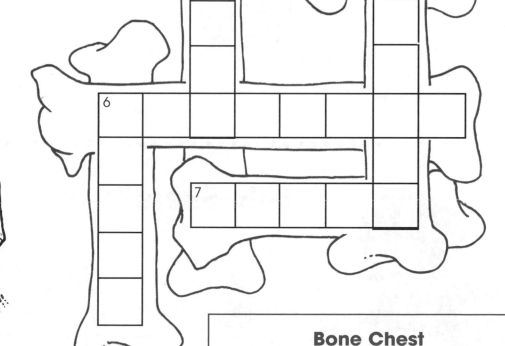

Bone Chest

ribs	toes	fingers
knee	skull	backbone
ankle	skeleton	

Rubber Bones

EXPERIMENT

The skeleton is a framework of 206 bones that has two important jobs: to hold up our bodies and to protect our insides. This means that bones must be healthy and strong. The outer part of bones is made of calcium which keeps bones strong. Ask your child what would happen if the calcium in his/her bones became weak. Have him/her try the experiment below to find out.

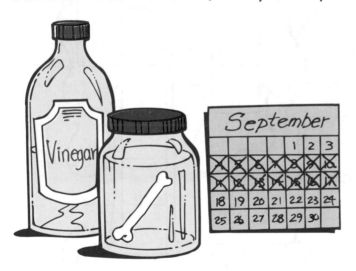

Directions:

1. Have your child clean a chicken bone and place it in a jar. Cover the bone with one cup of vinegar.

2. Have your child cover the jar tightly and let it sit for two weeks.

   After two weeks, discuss the following: How has the chicken bone changed? What would happen to your body without calcium?

Silly Skeletons

Have your child cut out the skeleton pieces on the next page. Have him/her use a reference book to piece the skeleton together on black paper.

Silly Skeletons

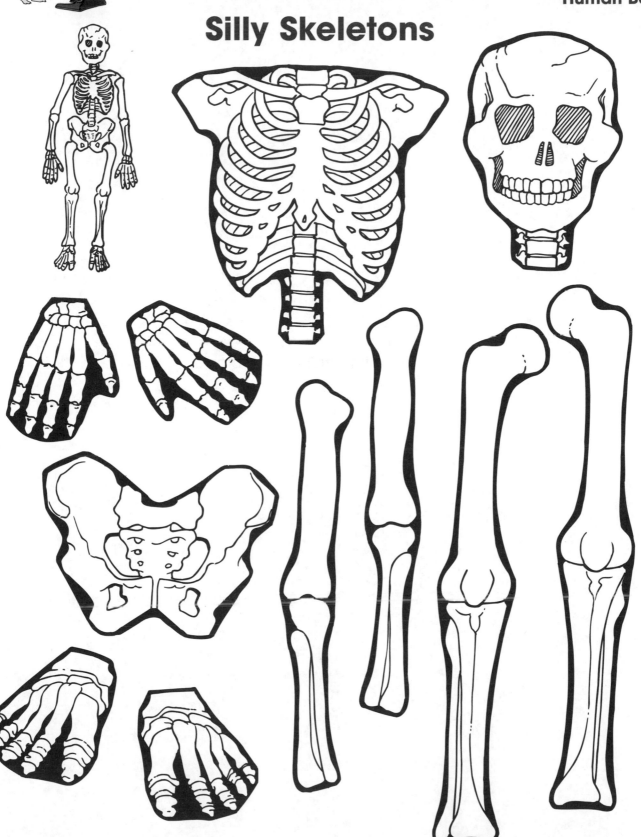

This page intentionally left blank.

Make a Model of You!

If you could look under your skin, what would you find?
You would find muscles, bones, a heart, a brain and many other body parts. Make a model of your insides to show where many of these parts are found.

Directions:

You will need someone to help you with the first step of your project.

1. Lie on your back on a large sheet of butcher paper. Turn your head so you are looking over your left shoulder.

2. Have your helper trace your outline with a pencil.

3. Use a dark crayon or marker and trace over the penciled outline.

4. Follow the directions on the following pages.

Name _____

Make a Model of You: Your Brain

My brain has a very important job. It must keep my body working day and night. My brain has three parts:

The **cerebrum** is the largest part of my brain. It does my thinking.

The **cerebellum** makes my muscles move smoothly.

The **brain stem** controls my breathing and the beating of my heart.

Directions:

1. Color the brain **gray**.

2. Cut out the brain.

3. Glue the brain to your paper body.

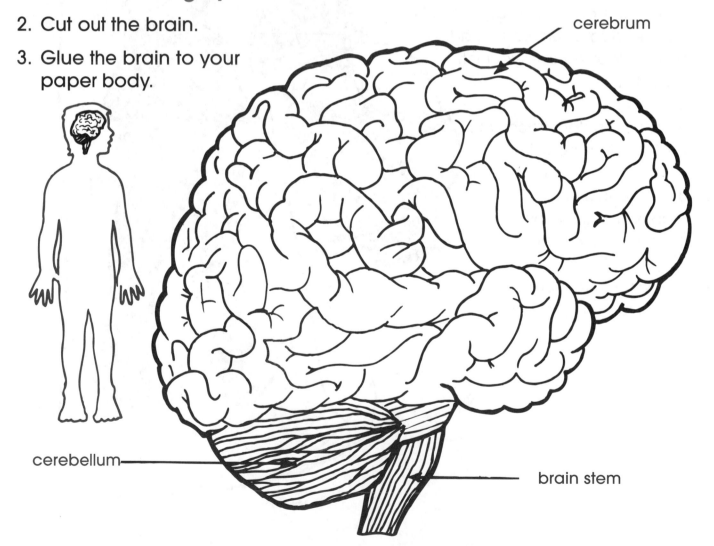

cerebrum

cerebellum

brain stem

Name _____

Make a Model of You: Your Stomach

My stomach is a kind of bag. It can hold about two pints of food. Food travels from my mouth to my stomach through a long tube, called the esophagus. Stomach juices mix with food to help digestion.

My stomach is found on the left side of my body. It is protected by my five lower ribs.

Directions:

1. Color your stomach **blue**.

2. Cut out your stomach and glue it to your paper body.

3. Draw a food tube (esophagus) from your stomach to your mouth. Color the food tube **brown**.

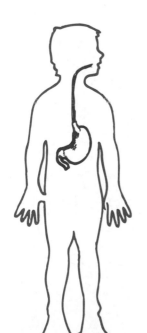

This page intentionally left blank.

Name _____

Make a Model of You: Your Intestines

Food is broken down in my small intestine. The nutrients are carried away by the blood in millions of small tubes. The leftover waste goes through my large intestine and out of my body.

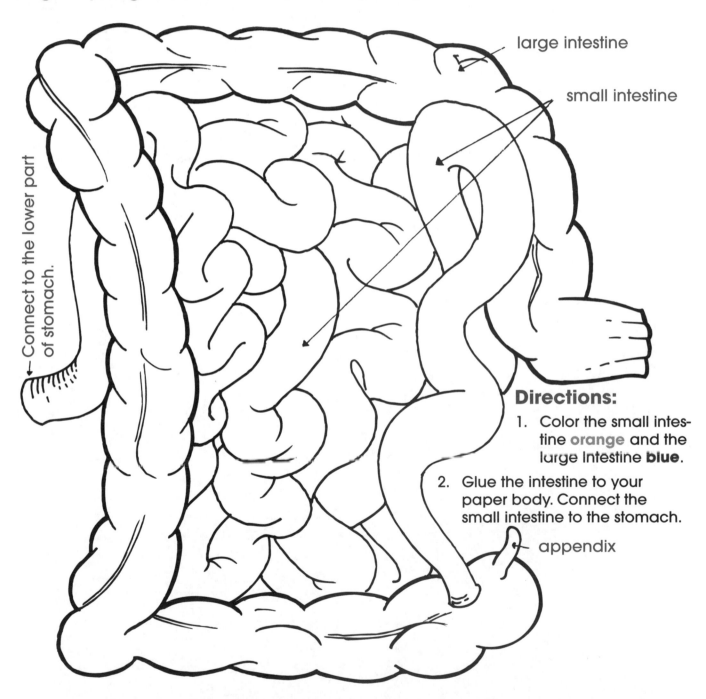

large intestine

small intestine

Connect to the lower part of stomach.

Directions:

1. Color the small intestine **orange** and the large intestine **blue**.

2. Glue the intestine to your paper body. Connect the small intestine to the stomach.

appendix

This page intentionally left blank.

Name _____

Make a Model of You: Your Lungs

My lungs take in the air that I breathe and give it to my blood. My blood takes it to all the cells in my body.

Directions:

1. On this page and the next, color the windpipe, bronchus and bronchioles **blue** and the lungs **red**.

2. Cut out the lungs on both pages.

3. Glue the left lung to the right lung on Tab A.

4. Bend and glue both Tabs B to your paper body. (Glue only the tabs.)

5. Draw a windpipe from the lungs to the mouth.

Tab B

windpipe

bronchus

bronchioles

Tab A

Right Lung

This page intentionally left blank.

Name _____

Make a Model of You: Your Lungs

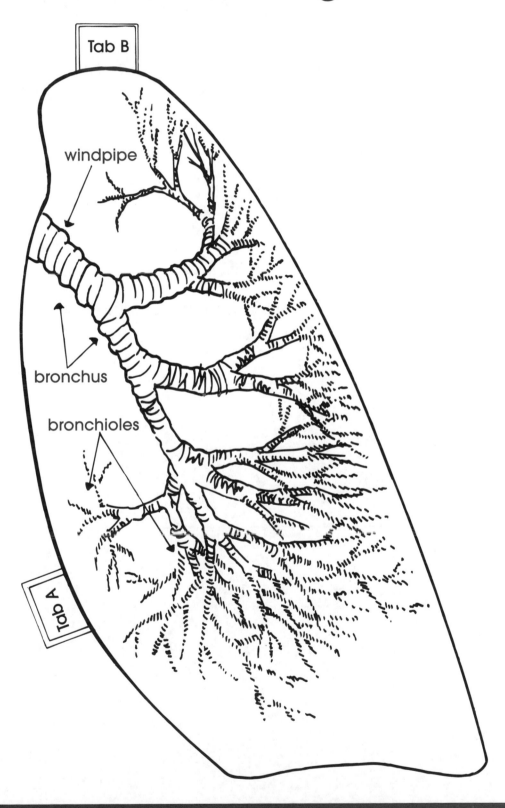

Tab B

windpipe

bronchus

bronchioles

Tab A

Left Lung

This page intentionally left blank.

Make a Model of You: Your Heart

My heart is a very strong pump. It pumps blood through more than 80,000 miles of tubes (arteries and veins) in my body. My heart is not very big. It is about the size of my fist and weighs less than one pound.

Directions:

1. Color the heart **red**.

2. Cut out the heart. Fold and glue the tabs to your paper body.

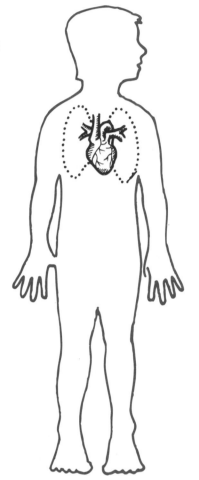

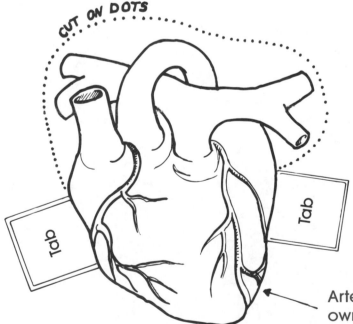

CUT ON DOTS

Tab

Tab

Arteries and veins give the heart its own supply of blood.

This page intentionally left blank.

Make a Model of You: Your Bones

My bones are very important. My arm bones and leg bones help me move. My skull and ribs protect the soft organs inside my body. Some of my bones make new blood cells for my body.

Directions:

1. Color the bones yellow.

2. Glue them to the right arm on your paper body.

This page intentionally left blank.

Name _____

Make a Model of You: Your Muscles

My muscles help my body move. They are connected to my bones with tendons. One muscle helps my arm bend, and the other one helps it to straighten out.

Directions:

1. Color the muscles **red**.

2. Cut out and glue the muscles to the bones on the right arm of your paper body.

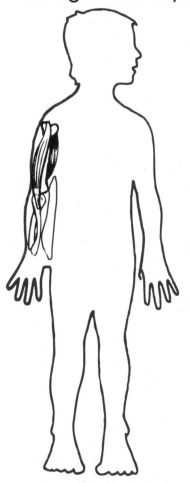

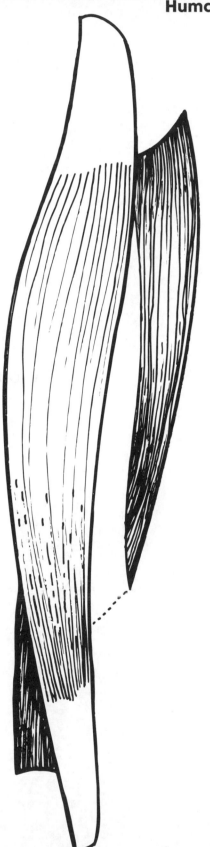

This page intentionally left blank.

Name _____

It Makes Sense to Me

We have five senses. We can see, hear, smell, taste and touch to help us understand and make "sense" of our world. Look at each group of pictures. Decide which sense you would use for most of the things in each group of pictures. Write the sense you would use on the line below each group. Then, draw an **X** on the one picture that **does not** belong in each group.

A "Sense"-ible Arrangement

Cut out the flowers at the bottom of the page. Pick one flower at a time, and look at the object and word on it. Paste the flower on the vase that tells which sense you would mainly use with the object on that flower.

Tummy Yummies

You will need:

1 cup of honey
1 cup of peanut butter
2 cups of dry milk
a measuring cup, a mixing bowl
spoons and wax paper

Help your child mix all of the ingredients
together. He/she can roll the mixture into balls
and set them on the wax paper for about an hour.
Enjoy this healthful treat together!

Brainfood Cookies

Eating oatmeal is a great way to get your brain going. It is a healthful
breakfast food that helps wake up your body after sleeping all night!

You will need:

1 stick of soft margarine
1 cup of oatmeal
$\frac{1}{2}$ cup of brown sugar
$\frac{1}{2}$ cup of flour
$\frac{1}{2}$ tsp of baking powder
measuring cups, mixing bowl,
mixing spoons, cookie sheets,
oven (preheat to 350°)

Help your child measure the ingredients and mix
them in the bowl. Then drop dough by spoonfuls
onto a cookie sheet and bake for ten minutes.
Let your child eat these delicious cookies . . . and
feed his/her brain!

Hokey Pokey

Music

Have your child sing the song "Hokey Pokey," substituting the body parts with new vocabulary from this unit. For example: "You put your ankle bone in, you put your ankle bone out. . . ."

Put your arm bone in and you shake it all about!

Be good to your teeth. BRUSH TWICE A DAY!

Healthful Habits

Drama

Use a video camera to create a short (one-minute) commercial advertising a healthful habit and telling the importance of forming that habit.

I'm One of a Kind

Art

Discuss the unique pattern of a person's fingerprints. Then, have your child press his/her fingers onto an ink pad and transfer his/her fingerprints onto paper. Your child can use crayons or markers to add details and create a picture. Let your child compare his/her fingerprints with the fingerprints of other family members.

Section 2
Nutrition

Food Pyramid

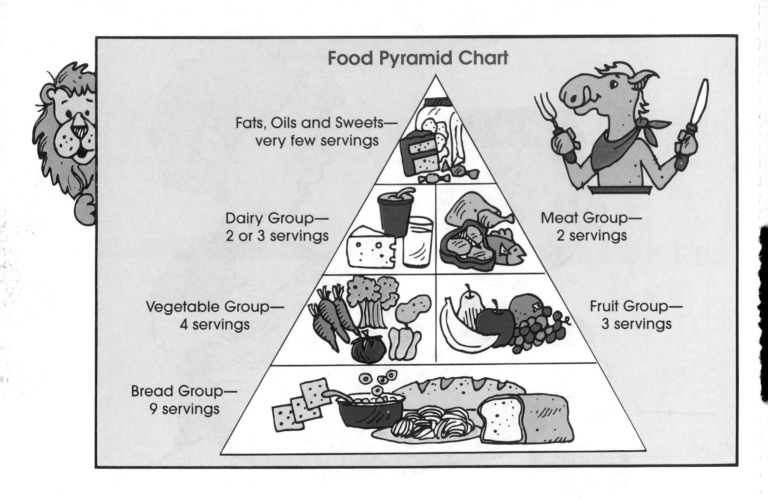

Food Pyramid Chart

Fats, Oils and Sweets—
very few servings

Dairy Group—
2 or 3 servings

Meat Group—
2 servings

Vegetable Group—
4 servings

Fruit Group—
3 servings

Bread Group—
9 servings

Name_____

Food Pyramid Graphing

Directions:

Use the graph and Food Pyramid Chart on the previous page to help you answer the questions.

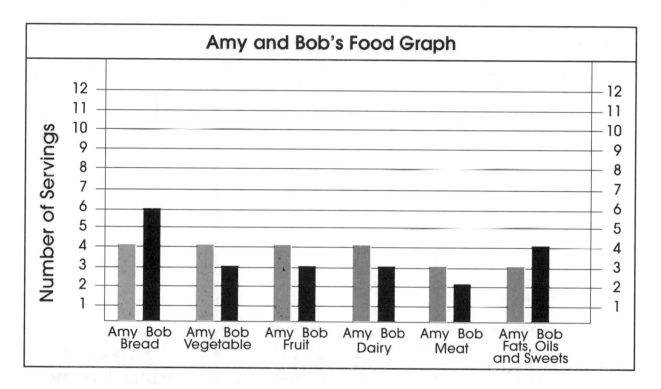

Amy and Bob's Food Graph

1. How many servings of bread did Bob eat? _____

2. How many **more** servings of vegetables did Amy eat than Bob? _____

3. Which person ate **fewer** servings of fruit? _____

4. How many servings of dairy did Amy have? _____

5. How many **fewer** servings of fruit did Bob eat than Amy? _____

6. Did Amy eat enough vegetables? _____

7. Did Bob and Amy eat enough fruit? _____

8. Amy and Bob should eat more from the _____ group.

Name_____

What's for Lunch?

We try to eat foods from the six food groups every day.
Take a close look at your lunch today.

List each of the foods from your lunch in the correct food groups.
Does your lunch include foods from all four of the food groups?

Bread Group	Fruits Group	Vegetable Group
Dairy Group	Meat Group	Fats, Oils and Sweets

The Big Six

It is important to eat foods from each of the six food groups every day.

Directions:

Cut out the food pictures. Glue them in the correct box.

Fruit Group	Vegetable Group	**Bread Group**
Dairy Group	**Meat Group**	**Fats, Oils and Sweets**

This page intentionally left blank.

Home Grain Inventory

Many of the foods that we eat come from grains. Take a close look at the foods made from grains in your kitchen.

Write the name of the food in the spaces below. Check the kind of grain it contains to the right.	barley	corn	oats	rice	soybeans	wheat

Pyramiding Foods

Read the names of the foods in the Word Bank. Write the food names on the lines under the correct food group.

Word Bank

carrots	cherries	
chicken	cheese	
fish	ham	cake
lettuce	bagel	oranges
pears	rolls	beans
toast	pie	yogurt
candy	bar	
cottage	cheese	

Dairy

Meats

Fruits

Sweets

Vege-tables

Grains

Section 3
Animals

This page intentionally left blank.

I'm Bigger Than You!

Animals are many different sizes. Color the pictures and cut them out.
Glue them on a sheet of paper in order from smallest to largest.

This page intentionally left blank.

Animals on the Go!

How do these animals move? Write **walk**, **fly** or **swim**.

_____

- - - - - - - - - - - - - - -

_____

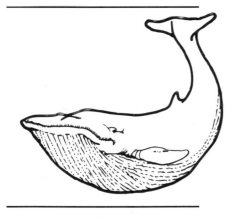

_____

- - - - - - - - - - - - - - -

_____

_____

- - - - - - - - - - - - - - -

_____

Name_____

Young Animals

Word Bank			
kitten	lamb	calf	puppy

Many young animals look like their parents. But some do not look like their parents. Draw a line from the parent to its young. Write the name of the young.

Stuffed Animal Sorting

After studying about various animals and their habitats, gather all the stuffed animals in your house. Create an animal corner with books and pictures of real animals. Then, sort the animals by their habitats.

Go Fish on a Farm!

Discuss the importance of farm animals and what they contribute to our dietary needs and to the farmers' needs. Talk about the reasons farmers may want these animals to reproduce. Then, introduce the game cards on pages 57 and 59.

Your child may use the cards to play the game "Go Fish!" after the cards have been cut out and colored. Be sure to tell your child that he/she will be matching adult animals with babies.

This page intentionally left blank.

Cards for "Go Fish on a Farm!"

hen   chick

dog   puppy

duck   duckling

sheep   lamb

farmer   child

This page intentionally left blank.

Name _____

Cards for "Go Fish on a Farm!"

pig

piglet

cat

kitten

cow

calf

goat

kid

horse

foal

This page intentionally left blank.

Animal Boxes

Directions:

In each box, write the name of at least two animals that fit the description. Use the animal names at the bottom of the page. Then, add other animals you know that fit each description!

insect	lays eggs	has no legs	has feathers
lives in water	farm animal	has a hard shell	has wings
runs fast	has horns or antlers	has scales	very slow
very strong	has hair	has long legs	is a good pet

Word Bank

butterfly	cow		horse	clam
giraffe	elephant	robin	beetle	cat
snail	turkey	deer	seal	bat
fish	bee	goat	moose	lion
turtle	pig	lizard	whale	hawk

This page intentionally left blank.

Animals in Winter

by _____

Directions:

Color and complete the following five pages. Cut them out.
Staple them together to make a book.

Active Animals

Directions:
Cut out the animals. Glue them in place.

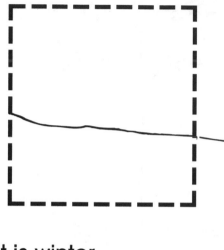

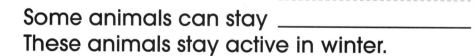

It is winter.
Deep snow covers the ground.

_____

Some animals can find _____ .

_____

Some animals can stay _____ .
These animals stay active in winter.

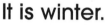

Word Bank
food
warm

Hibernation

Directions: Cut out the fat woodchuck. Glue him by his hole. Trace the path to the woodchuck's home.

Some animals hibernate in the winter.

The woodchuck grows a layer of _____ in the fall.

His heartbeat slows _____ . His body temperature

goes _____ . He stays in his home while it is _____ .

Word Bank
cold
fat
down
down

Storing Food

Directions: Cut out the beaver. Glue him by the hole in the ice.
Trace the path to the beaver's lodge.

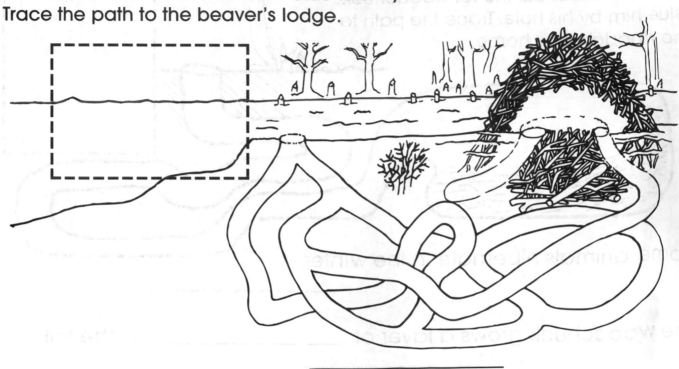

Some animals store food for _____.

The beaver stores food in his _____.

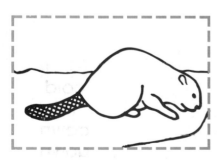

Migration

Directions:

Cut out the animals. Glue them in place.

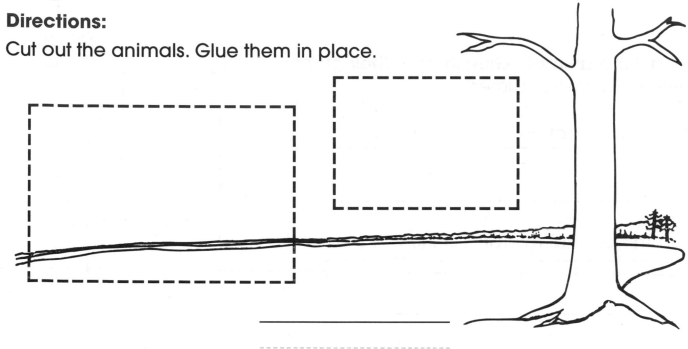

It is hard to find _____ in the winter.

It is hard to stay _____ in the winter.

Some animals move to warmer places.
This is called migration.

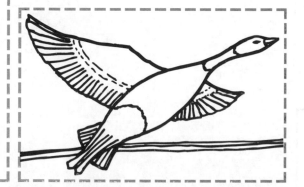

Word Bank
warm
food

Animals in Winter

Directions:

Cut out the animals. Glue them in their places.
Write the animals' names.

This animal hibernates in winter.

This animal migrates in the winter.

This animal stays active in the winter.

This animal stores food for the winter.

Word Bank
rabbit
bird
beaver
woodchuck

Interesting Invertebrates

Invertebrates are animals that have no backbone or inside skeleton. Some have soft bodies protected by shells. Others have soft bodies that are not protected. Some invertebrates are so small that they can only be seen by a microscope.

Below are some examples of invertebrates.
Use the clues to name each one.

___ ___ ___ ___ ___ I P E D E

S ___ ___ ___ ___   F ___ ___ ___

E ___ ___ ___ ___   W ___ ___ ___

J ___ ___ ___ ___ ___

F ___ ___ ___

S ___ ___ ___

D ___ ___ ___ ___

S ___ ___ ___ ___ ___

S ___ ___   C ___ ___ ___ ___ ___ ___

Insects

What Is an Insect?

All insects have three main body parts: head, thorax and abdomen. On the head are the eyes, mouth and antennae. The legs and wings are attached to the thorax. The abdomen is the part at the rear of the body. Insects have six legs. Most insects have two types of eyes. Compound eyes are the larger eyes. Compound eyes see color and movement. Between the compound eyes are the simple eyes. Simple eyes are sensitive to light and dark. Insects have antennae on top of their heads which are used to feel, to smell, and in some insects, to hear.

Show your child the pattern of the insect on page 71. Show your child where all the body segments are located, and let him/her color the insect.

This is an insect.

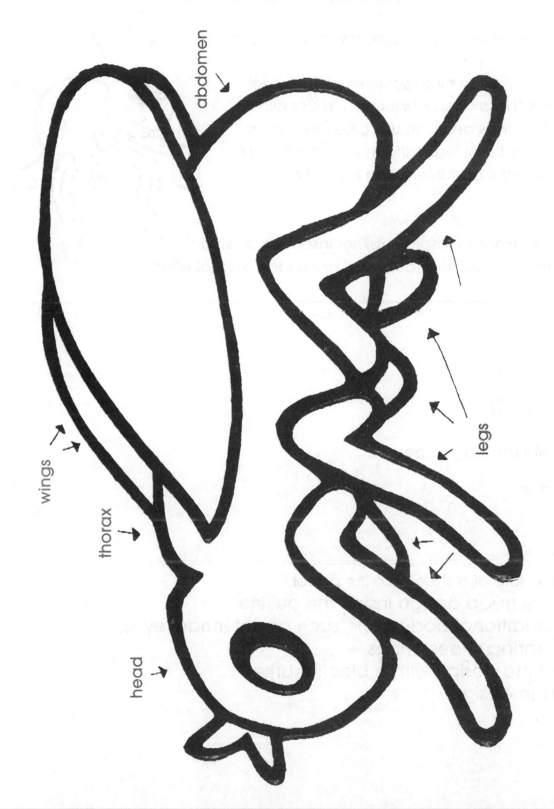

abdomen

legs

wings

thorax

head

Interesting Insects

Let your child create his/her own insect! Give your child scrap fabric, construction paper and anything else you can find to make the three sections of the insect's body (head, thorax and abdomen). Your child will want to add wings and can use pipe cleaners to make the insect's six legs (attached to the thorax). Hang this colorful and interesting insect from your ceiling.

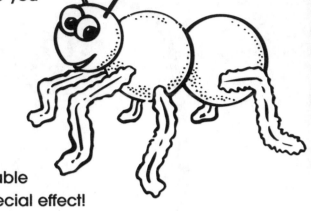

If your child wishes to display his/her insect on a table top, he/she can add real rocks and grass for a special effect!

Shoe Fly

You will need:

shoe
9" x 12" white drawing paper
pencil
black marker
crayons

Directions:

1. Trace the sole of a shoe onto the paper.
2. Draw the tread design inside the outline.
3. Draw additional body parts, such as antennae, eyes, feet wearing shoes, wings.
4. Outline the design with a black marker.
5. Color the design.

Insect Cages

Insect "Indoor" Home:

This insect cage is easy to make.

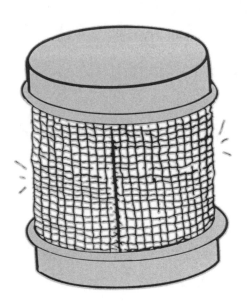

Directions:

Roll copper wire screen to fit two aluminum cake pans. Join the edges of the screen by sewing them together with a single strand of copper wire removed from the cut edge. Add the cake pans to form the top and bottom of the cage. Remove the top to put insects into the cage.

Ant Farm:

You will need:

a one-gallon jar
soil
dark paper
cotton
cheesecloth

Directions:

Fill the jar about halfway to the top with soil. Find an ant hill. Use a shovel to lift the ant hill and the surrounding dirt and debris into the jar. Cover the jar with dark paper to encourage the ants to make tunnels. Place some cotton on top of the dirt and put a little water on it every few days. Cover the top with cheesecloth. Then, punch holes in the lid for air and screw on the lid. Feed the ants crumbs of bread, honey or sugar water.

Insects

Do the puzzle about insects.
Color the insects.

Word Bank

skeleton   legs   wings   three   eyes

Across:

3. Insects have three pair of _____.

4. Insects have _____ main body sections.

Down:

1. Insects have a hard outer _____.

2. Many insects have two pair of _____.

5. Insects have different kinds of _____.

A Ladybug Lunch

Make a delicious "ladybug" snack!

You will need:

1 apple cut in half
10 seedless grapes
2 lettuce leaves
2 T peanut butter
6–10 raisins
7 toothpicks

Directions:

1. Wash and pat dry the lettuce.
2. Set the lettuce on a plate and put half of the apple on top of the lettuce, skin-side up.
3. Use the peanut butter to stick the raisins on the "ladybug's" back so that they look like her "spots."
4. The toothpicks are used to place the grape on as the "head" and for the "legs."
5. Eat your little friend. . . . Yummy!

Insects

Directions:

Cut out the monarch butterfly. Glue it in place.
Color the insects.

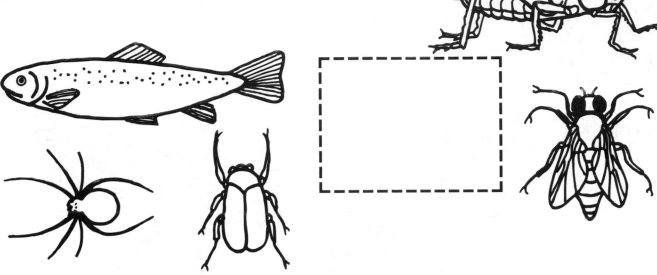

_____

The monarch butterfly is an _____ .

_____

It has six _____ .

_____

It has _____ body parts.

Word Bank
insect
three
legs

The Butterfly

by _____

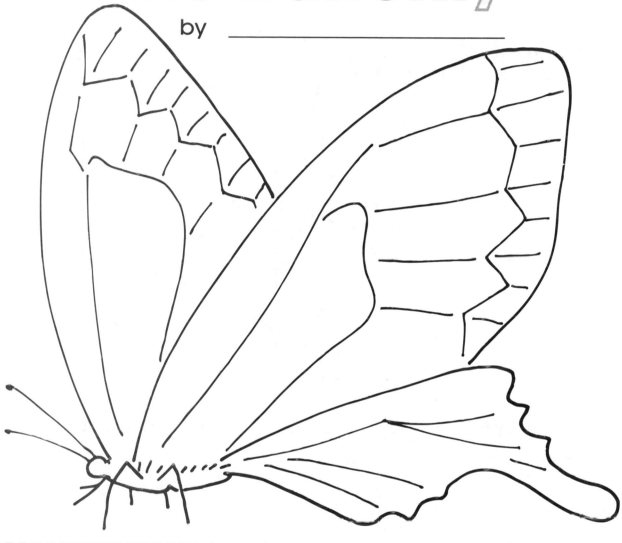

Directions:

Color and complete the following seven pages.
Cut them out. Staple them together to make a book.

The Egg

Directions:

Cut out the butterfly. Cut out the egg.
Glue each one on a milkweed leaf.

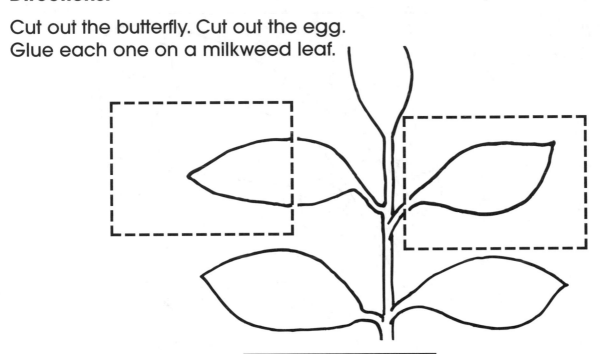

The butterfly lays one _____ on a milkweed

_____

_____ .

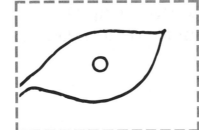

**Word
Bank**
leaf
egg

The Caterpillar

Directions:

Color the caterpillar black, white and yellow.
Cut out the caterpillar. Glue it on the milkweed leaf.

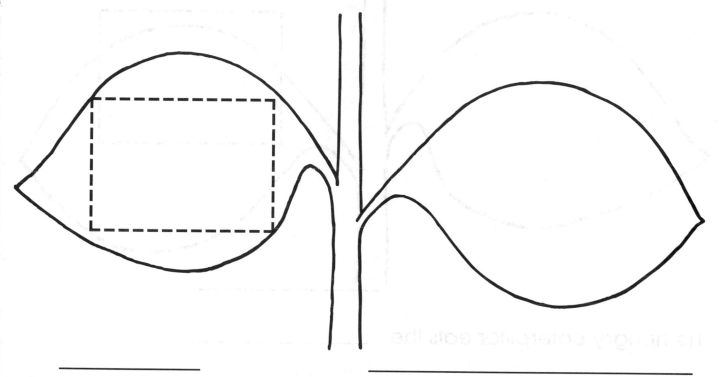

_____   _____

The <u>hatches into a</u>   .   _____

 -

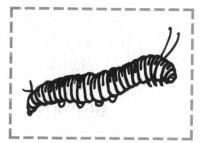

**Word
Bank
egg
caterpillar**

Growing

Directions:

Cut out the caterpillar and its food.
Glue them on the milkweed plant.

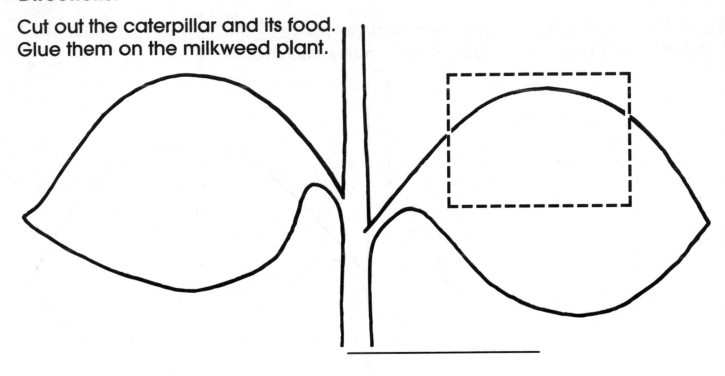

The hungry caterpillar eats the _____ .

The caterpillar is   .

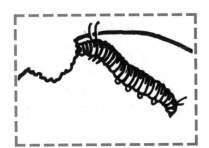

Word Bank
leaf
growing

The Chrysalis

Directions:

Cut out the chrysalis.
Glue it in place.

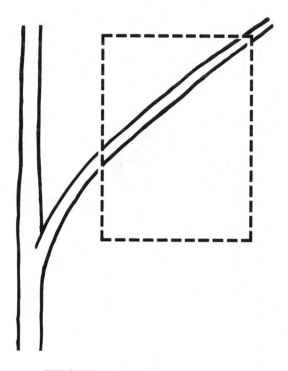

The caterpillar is ready to _____ .

It forms a pale _____ chrysalis.

Word Bank
green
change

The Butterfly

Directions:

Cut out the butterfly.
Glue it in place.

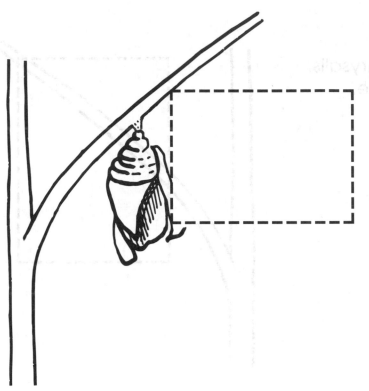

_____

The _____ is now a butterfly.

_____

The _____ flies away.

Word Bank
butterfly
caterpillar

Metamorphosis

Directions:

Show how the monarch
butterfly changes.
Cut out the pictures.
Glue them in order.

4	1
3	2

**Word
Bank**

butterfly

The life cycle of a _____
is called metamorphosis.

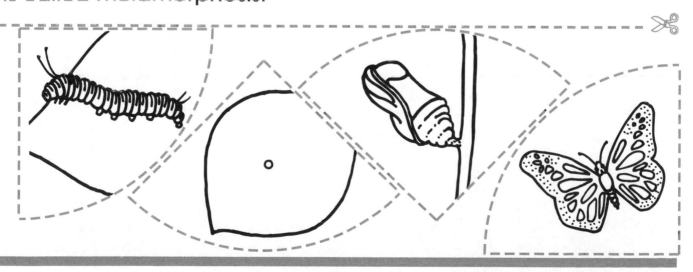

This page intentionally left blank.

From the Inside Out

Animals whose skeletons have backbones are called vertebrates. The backbone, or spine, is made up of bones called vertebrae.

Directions: Look at the skeletons below. Use the riddle and the Word Bank to write the name of each vertebrate.

1.

I stand tall and proud, so please don't ask me to eat from the ground.

I am a _____.

5.

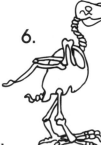

I am thankful to be alive at holidays. People might "gobble" me up!

I am a _____.

2.

I have wings, but I cannot fly. I love to strut around in my "tuxedo."

I am a _____.

6.

They say I have no hair, and they're right. I represent a great country.

I am a _____.

3.

I am not a bird, but I can fly. Some people think I am "blind."

I am a _____.

4.

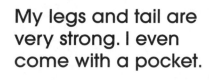

My legs and tail are very strong. I even come with a pocket.

I am a _____.

Word Bank

bald eagle
kangaroo
turkey
penguin
giraffe
bat

Amazing Amphibians

Amphibians are cold-blooded vertebrates (animals with backbones). They have no scales on their skin. Most amphibians hatch from eggs laid in water or on damp ground. Many amphibians grow legs as they develop into adults. Some live on land and have both lungs and gills for breathing. Frogs and toads are examples of amphibians.

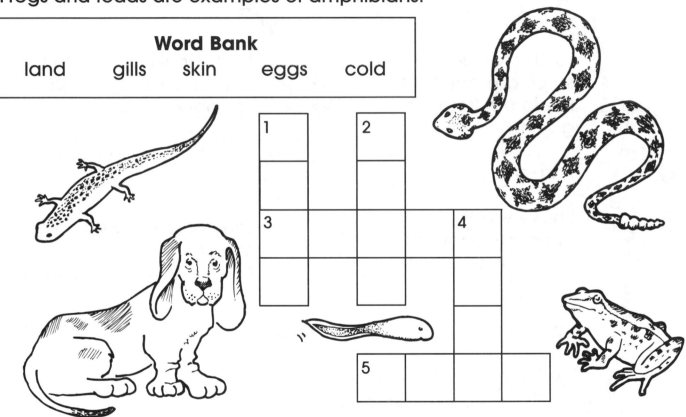

Word Bank

land   gills   skin   eggs   cold

Do the puzzle about amphibians. Color the amphibians.

Across:

3. Amphibian babies breathe with either lungs or _____.

5. Amphibians live in the water and on _____.

Down:

1. Amphibian babies usually hatch from _____.

2. Amphibians are _____-blooded animals.

4. Amphibians often have smooth, moist _____.

The Frog

by _____

✂ -

Directions:

Color and complete the following five pages.
Cut them out. Staple them together to make a book.

Laying Eggs

Directions:

Cut out the frog's eggs.
Glue them in the water.

The frog lays her _____ in the spring.

She lays the eggs in the _____ .

 -

Word Bank
water
eggs

Tadpoles

Directions:

Cut out the tadpole.
Glue it in the water.

The frog's eggs hatch into _____ .

They breathe with _____ like fish.

✂ -

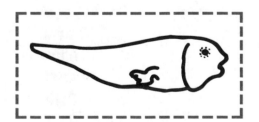

Word Bank
gills
tadpoles

Growing

Directions: Cut out the changing tadpole. Glue it in the water.

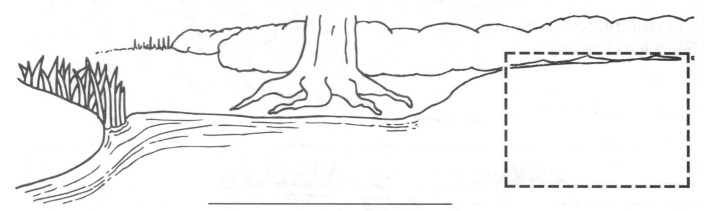

_____

The tadpole grows _____ .

_____

Its _____ becomes smaller.

_____

The tadpole still lives in the _____ .

_____

It can live on land when it becomes a _____ .

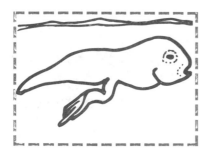

**Word
Bank**
tail
water
legs
frog

The Life Cycle of a Frog

Directions:

Color and cut out the pictures.
Glue them in order. Write the name
of each picture.

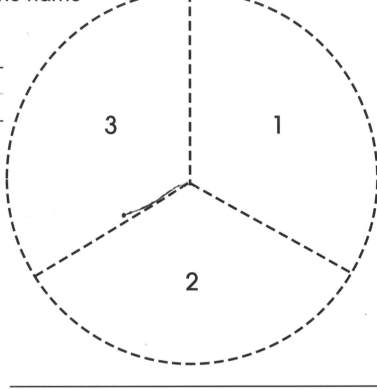

3

1

2

**Word
Bank**
egg
adult
tadpole

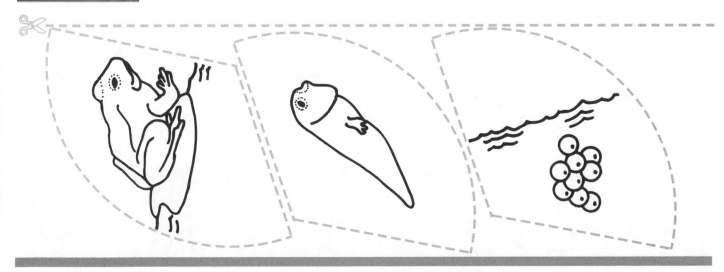

91

This page intentionally left blank.

Fishy Facts

Fish live almost anywhere there is water. Although fish come in many different shapes, colors and sizes, they are alike in many ways.

- All fish have backbones.
- Most fish have fins.
- Fish breathe with gills.
- Many fish have scales and fairly tough skin.
- Most fish are cold-blooded.

Check out and read books about fish to discover more facts about fish. As your child discovers new facts about fish, print the facts on the fish shapes on the following page and attach them to a display board. Your child can use the above facts to get him/her started.

This page intentionally left blank.

Name_____

Fishy Facts Patterns

This page intentionally left blank.

Name_____

Fabulous Fish

Fish are cold-blooded animals who live in the sea and in fresh water. They use their gills to breathe underwater. A fish's body is covered with scales. They use fins to move.

Word Bank				
water	scales	cold	fins	gills

Do the puzzle about fish. Color the fish.

Across:

2. Fish breathe through _____.
4. A fish is a _____-blooded animal.
5. Fish live in the sea and fresh _____.

Down:

1. Fish have _____, not legs.

3. A fish's body is often covered with _____.

Inside and Outside

Directions:

Use the words to label the fish below. Explain to your child that of all the animals with backbones, only fish and tadpoles have gills. Tell him/her that fish breathe through their gills.

Word Bank					
gills	mouth	eye	nostril	fins	backbone

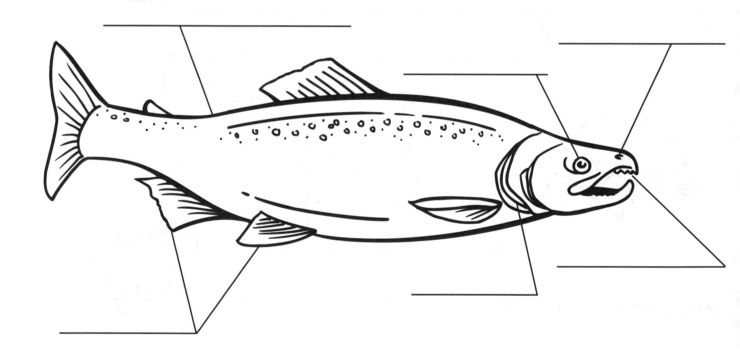

Name_____

The Reptile House

There are about 6,000 different kinds of **reptiles**. They come in all shapes and colors. Their sizes in length range from 2 inches to almost 30 feet. Reptiles can be found on every continent except Antarctica. Even though reptiles can seem quite different, they all . . .

- breathe with lungs.
- are cold-blooded.
- have dry, scaly skin.
- have a backbone.

In the Reptile House at the zoo, each animal needs to be placed in the correct area. Read the information about each reptile. Then, use the clues and the pictures to write the name of each reptile in its area.

Giant Tortoise can live over 100 years. It can hide under its shell for protection.

Reticulated Python is the longest snake. One was almost 33 feet long.

Saltwater Crocodile is one of the largest reptiles. It can weigh 1,000 lbs.

Komodo Dragon is a dragon-like reptile. It is the largest living lizard.

Tuatara is closely related to the extinct dinosaur.

Clues:

- The snake is between the largest lizard and the largest member of the turtle family.

- A relative of the alligator is on the far right side.

- The reptile who carries its "house" is in the middle.

Turtle Time

Help your child use resource materials to learn about marine and land turtles. Be sure he/she understands that they are reptiles. Show your child a live box turtle (or a picture of one). Point out that it has tough, scaled feet with claws. Its body is like a rectangular prism. Then, show him/her pictures of sea turtles. Although they can be huge—a leatherback can weigh up to 1,500 pounds—their bodies are sleek for moving through the water. Their limbs are flat and wide for swimming.

Pour three or four gallons of water into an empty aquarium. Then, let your child immerse one hand in the water with fingers apart and try to pull through the water. Second, with his/her fingers and thumb closed and cupped, have your child try to pull through the water. Ask him/her which way is more successful (the second is). Explain to him/her that the advantage of having flippers enables marine turtles to swim well. Ask what any disadvantages might be. (Hint: Turtles lay eggs on land.)

Allow your child to push a rectangular wooden block, representing the box turtle, through the water. Then, compare that to the ease of pushing a thinner, sleeker piece of wood, representing the sea turtle, through the water. Discuss with him/her how these adaptations benefit the turtles.

Extension: Show your child pictures of ichthyosaurs and plesiosaurs, dinosaurs that had some of the same characteristics as sea turtles.

Name_____

Reptiles

Do the puzzle about reptiles.
Color the reptiles.

Word Bank
eggs   cold   scales
snake   turtle

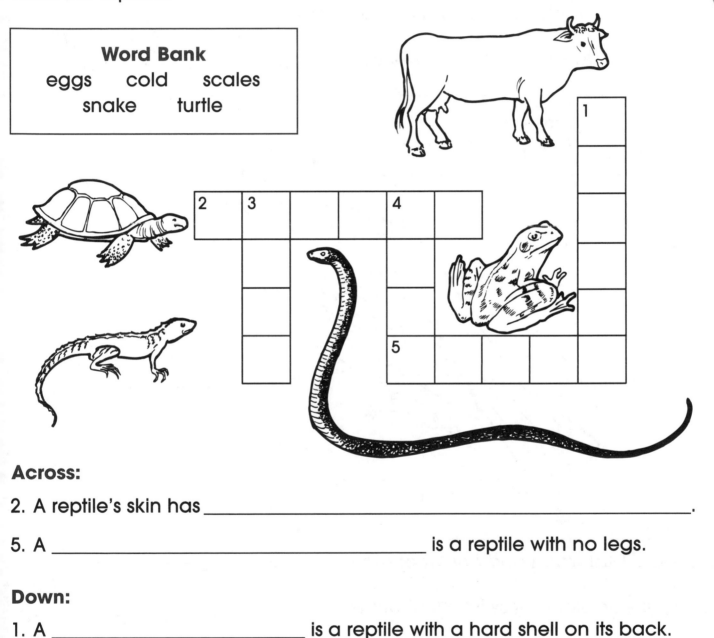

Across:

2. A reptile's skin has _____.

5. A _____ is a reptile with no legs.

Down:

1. A _____ is a reptile with a hard shell on its back.

3. Reptiles are _____-blooded animals.

4. Baby reptiles hatch from _____.

Name_____

Feathered Friends

Birds are warm-blooded vertebrates (animals with backbones). They are unique animals, because their bodies are covered with feathers. Instead of front legs or arms, birds have wings and most can fly.

Directions: Read the riddle. Name each bird part.

Word Bank

feathers   feet   bill   wings

I keep a bird warm and dry. What am I?_____

I help a bird stand or swim. What am I? _____

I help a bird eat. What am I? _____

I help a bird fly high in the sky. What am I? _____

Name_____

Birds

Do the puzzle about birds.
Color the birds.

| Word Bank |
| feathers   bill   lungs   eggs   warm |

Across:

2. A bird is a _____-blooded animal.

3. Baby birds are hatched from _____.

5. Birds breathe with their _____.

Down:

1. _____ keep a bird's body warm and dry.

4. A bird uses its _____ to pick up food.

That's for the Birds!

Help your child use the following materials and rebus directions to make a bird feeder:

You will need:

newspaper, plastic knife, string, pine cone, peanut butter, birdseed

Rebus Directions:

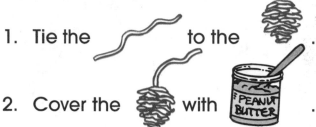

1. Tie the _____ to the _____ .

2. Cover the _____ with _____ .

3. Roll the _____ in _____ .

4. Tie the _____ to a _____ .

A Feathery Flock

Have your child cut out the bird pattern on the next page and lay it on a folded 12" x 18" sheet of colored construction paper, matching the folds. Then, trace around the pattern and cut it out. Your child can make the bird "fly" by holding it by its belly and opening the fold at the place marked with the star. Bring the open pieces all the way under the bird's body and over its head. Its wings should now be open. You child may glue craft feathers on the bird, punch a hole in it and hang it from the ceiling using string or yarn.

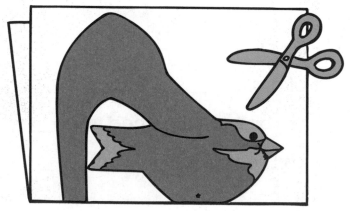

Name_____

Bird Pattern

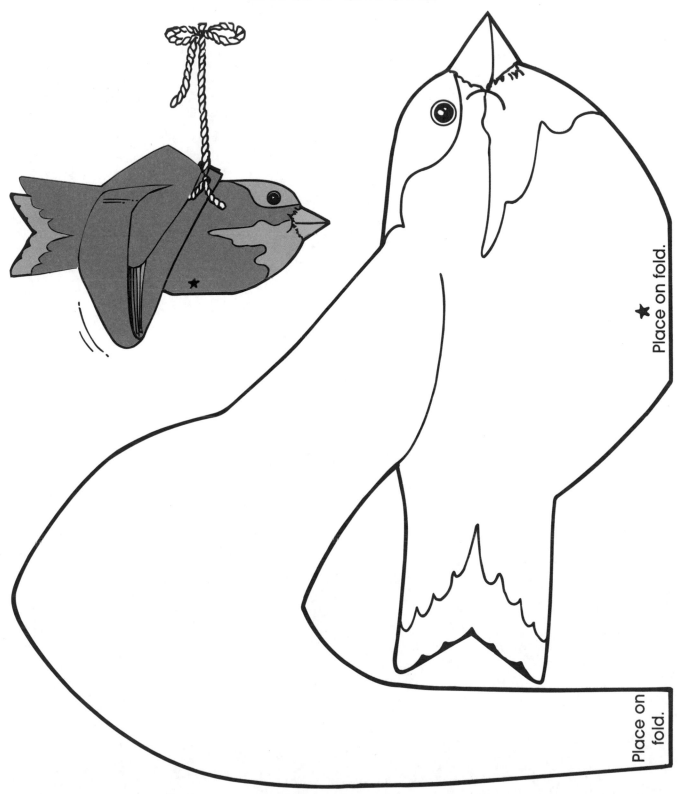

Place on fold.

★ Place on fold.

Place on fold.

This page intentionally left blank.

My Bird List

Bird watchers keep a list of the different kinds of birds they have seen. They also keep track of the date and location. Begin a list of your own using the chart below.

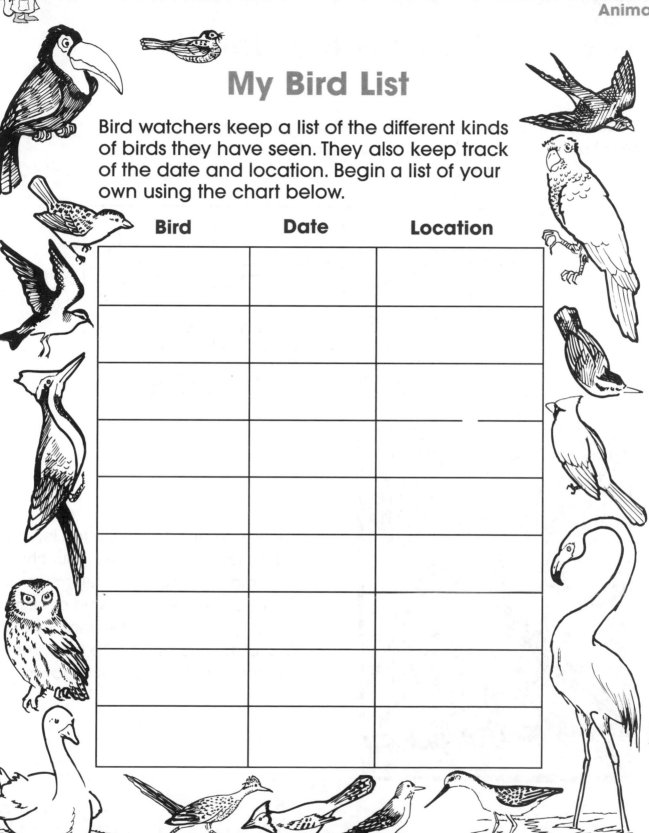

Bird	Date	Location

The Early Bird Gets the Worm!

Directions:

1. Discuss the three types of bird beaks. Explain how each type has functions similar to the tool listed. Let your child experiment with the tools.

SHAPE			
FOOD	small animals (meat)	flower nectar	seeds, worms
TOOL	pincers (grasp and tear)	straw (sucking action)	pliers (pick and pull)

2. Draw a large beak in the top left portion of a sheet of paper. Have your child use informational books to determine which types of birds have the kind of beak on the paper. Then, he/she can draw the rest of the bird's body. Do the same for all three beak types shown above.

Tasty Bird Nests

Help your child follow the directions below to make a tasty snack which looks like a bird's nest!

You will need:

wax paper
1 bag of butterscotch or
    chocolate chips
1 5-ounce can of chow mein
    noodles
1 cup of peanuts
1 small bag of jelly beans

Directions:

1. Melt the chips.
2. Stir in the noodles and peanuts.
3. Drop spoonfuls of the mixture onto the wax paper. Have your child mold the mixture into a "nest" shape.
4. Have him/her add jellybean "eggs" and chill the creation for 15 minutes.
5. Let your child gobble up these tasty bird nests!

Marvelous Mammals

Mammals are warm-blooded vertebrates (animals with backbones) who use lungs to breathe. Mammals give birth to live babies and feed their babies milk. Most mammals have fur or hair on their bodies. Cats, horses and humans are examples of mammals.

Do the puzzle about mammals.
Color the mammals.

Word Bank
hair   babies
lungs   milk
warm

Across:

2. A mammal's body is usually covered with _____.

3. Mother mammals feed _____ to their babies.

5. Mammals' _____ are born alive.

Down:

1. Mammals are _____-blooded.

4. Mammals breathe with _____.

Whales

Tell your child that there are two types of whales—toothed and baleen. Blue, gray and humpbacks are baleen whales. They have hundreds of thin plates that hang down from the tops of their upper jaws. The whales open their mouths and draw in plankton (tiny sea plants and animals) and water. Next, they squeeze out the water with their tongues, leaving the plankton trapped by the baleen. Finally, they eat the plankton.

To demonstrate to your child how the baleen works, hold a strainer above a pail or dishpan. Mix "plankton" (alfalfa sprouts) into a quart of water. Pour the mixture through the strainer. The sprouts are left in the strainer just as the plankton is captured by the whale's baleen.

Whale Pop-Ups

Let your child try writing riddles using facts about whales. Then, he/she can make a pop-up book. Help your child fold a sheet of 9" x 12" light blue construction paper in half. Then, he/she can cut two one-inch slits, an inch apart, on the fold. (This will be the tab.) Next, have him/her write a riddle using clues for a specific whale on the front of the folded construction paper and decorate it. Your child can then create a whale using gray, black and/or white construction paper, and glue it to the tab that has been pushed to the inside. Finally, have your child write the name of the whale below it.

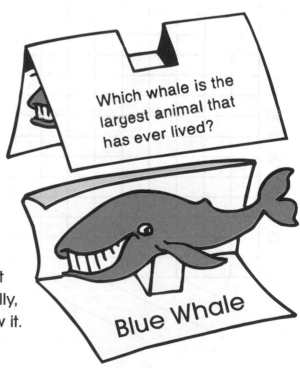

Which whale is the largest animal that has ever lived?

Blue Whale

Whale Graph

Help your child use resource materials to find the lengths of whales to graph. Record the information on paper. (For your convenience, a list of some whales and their lengths has been included below.) Discuss how to record the information gathered about whales on the bar graph. Then, let your child work independently to create a graph.

Extension: List the whales from shortest to longest. Note: The whales listed below can grow to the number of feet listed.

Whale Lengths:
blue – 100 feet   **sperm** – 65 feet   **bowhead** – 60 feet   **gray** – 50 feet
humpback – 50 feet   **killer** – 30 feet   **pilot** – 28 feet   **narwhal** – 18 feet

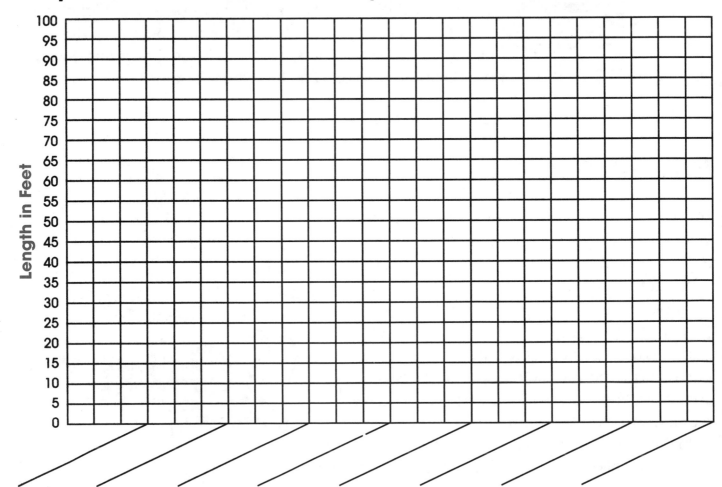

Whale of a Game

Use the whale identification cards to play a game of whale dominoes. Cut out the whale pictures and directions below. Keep all of the game pieces in a resealable plastic bag.

To Play with a Partner:

This game is played like dominoes. Spread out the whale cards face-down. Each player draws four cards. A player having a card containing two of the same whale begins by laying out that card face-up and naming the whale. (If neither player has a double whale, take turns drawing from the center pile until one can begin the game.) Then, the second player adds a matching card. If he/she does not have one, he/she draws a card from the center pile and loses a turn. Play continues until one person has used all of his/her whale cards.

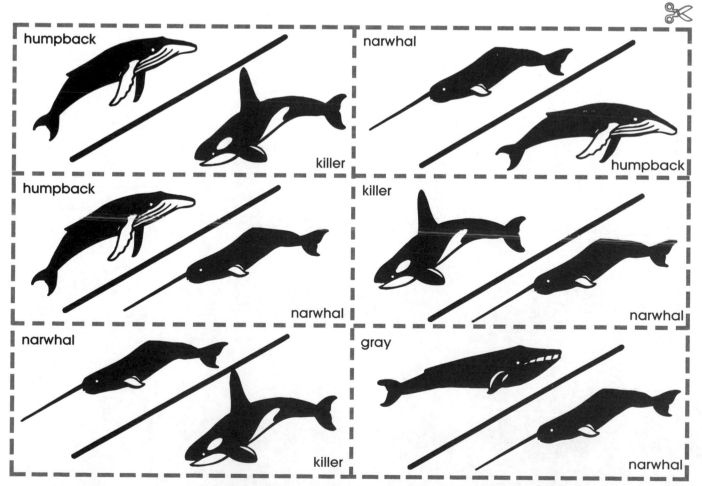

This page intentionally left blank.

Whale Cards

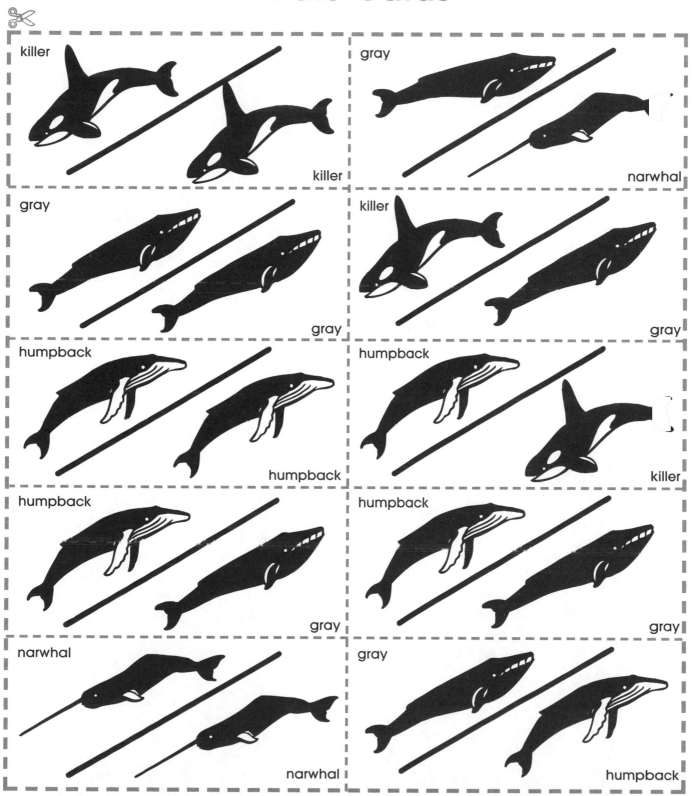

This page intentionally left blank.

All in the Family

Directions: Draw an **X** on the animal that does not belong.

1.

2.

3.

4.

5.

Riddle Me This!

Directions: Circle the animal that does not belong in the group.
Print the letters beside the circled words in the spaces
below to find the answer to the riddle.

Birds
1. L robin
   N bluebird
   I cow
   J crow

Insects
2. L snake
   A ladybug
   N wasp
   T bee

Dogs
3. B collie
   I beagle
   S shepherd
   L ox

Reptiles
4. R snake
   I horse
   G turtle
   W alligator

Farm Animals
5. G tiger
   K pig
   O cow
   Y hen

Jungle Animals
6. J lion
   B cheetah
   U tiger
   A rat

Zoo Animals
7. M bear
   O giraffe
   T dog
   F zebra

Ocean Animals
8. H octopus
   T whale
   K shark
   O camel

Fish
9. R raccoon
   I perch
   V catfish
   L tuna

Riddle:
What do you call a sick crocodile?

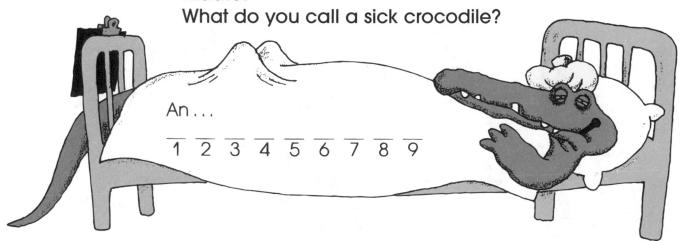

An . . .

___ ___ ___ ___ ___ ___ ___ ___ ___
 1   2   3   4   5   6   7   8   9

Name_____

Animals at Home

Have you ever seen a fish living in a tree?
Of course you haven't!
Fish live in the water.
Help the animals find their homes.

Directions:

Color the picture.
Cut out each animal.
Glue it on its home.

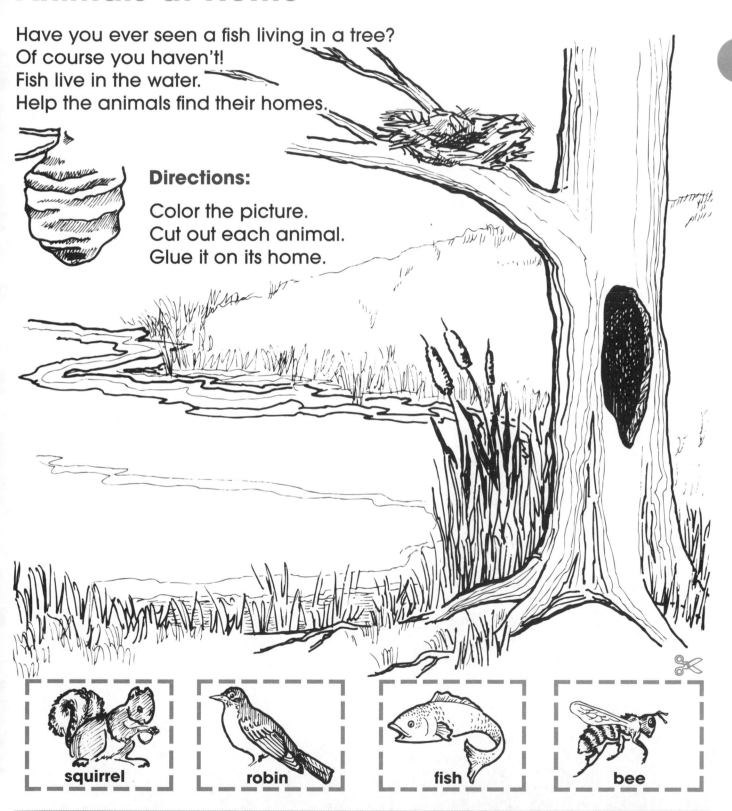

squirrel   **robin**   **fish**   **bee**

This page intentionally left blank.

At Home in the Forest Community

Many animals make their homes in a forest community, but some of the animals in this picture do not belong.

Directions: Draw an **X** on the animals that **do not** belong.

Desert Dwellers

Directions:

1. Discuss the warm, dry climate of most deserts. Share several books that illustrate the plant and animal life there. Discuss the different ways plants and animals have adapted to life with very little water.

2. Have your child turn a shoe box on its side and cover the "walls" with construction paper so that the box resembles the warm habitat of the desert.

3. Have your child color and cut out the desert animals on pages 123 and 125. Bend back the tabs, apply the glue and place the animals. Once the animals are in place, have your child completely cover the bottom of the box with glue and sprinkle sand over it.

Desert Dweller Patterns

Bobcat

Glue Here

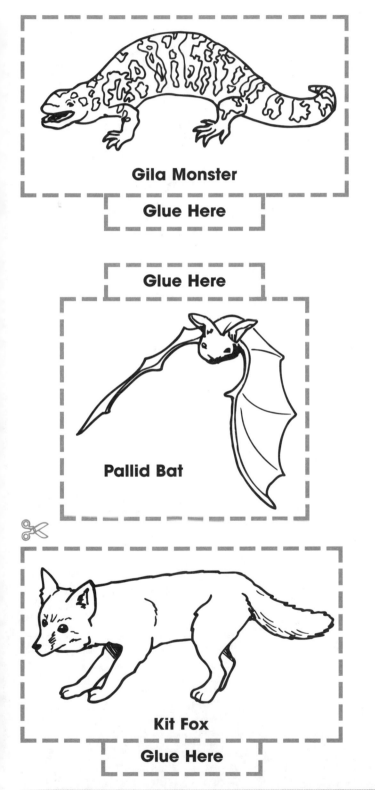

Gila Monster

Glue Here

Glue Here

Pallid Bat

Camel

Glue Here

Kit Fox

Glue Here

Elf Owl

Glue Here

This page intentionally left blank.

Desert Dwellers Patterns

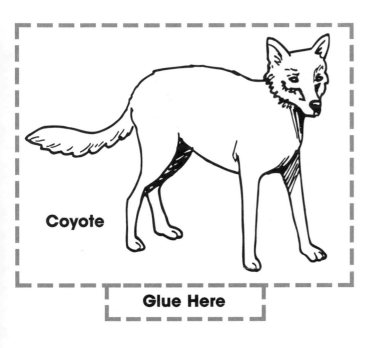

Coyote

Glue Here

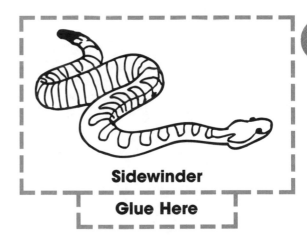

Sidewinder

Glue Here

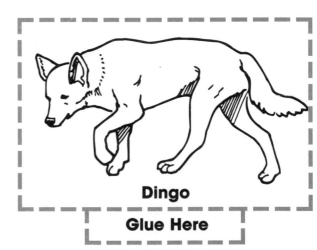

Dingo

Glue Here

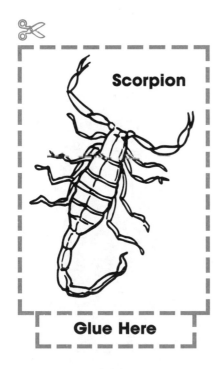

Scorpion

Glue Here

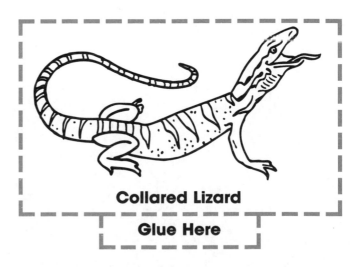

Collared Lizard

Glue Here

This page intentionally left blank.

Grassland Animals

Help your child create a grassland habitat.

You will need:

one 9" x 9" piece of tagboard
one 2" x 9" strip of green construction paper
one 3" x 9" strip of brown construction paper
one 4" x 9" strip of yellow construction paper
grass, pebbles and small twigs (gathered from outside), glue, scissors, crayons, scrap paper

Discuss various zoo animals that originally lived in a grassland habitat. (See Word Bank below.) Provide several books and tapes to help your child

create a long list of grassland dwellers. Then, give your child the tagboard and a copy of the animals on the next two pages. Have him/her color them, cut them out and glue them so that they stand upright on his/her board.

Have your child take one strip of green, yellow and brown paper and cut slits to create various heights of grass. Have him/her glue the grass to the tagboard. Finally, cover the remaining exposed tagboard with the grass, pebbles and twigs you gathered from outside.

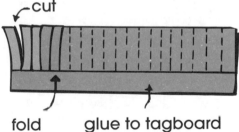

cut

fold   glue to tagboard

Word Bank
hippopotamus
elephant   rhinoceros
giraffe   kangaroo
aardvark   zebra
prairie dog   kudu
lion   ostrich

This page intentionally left blank.

Grassland Animal Patterns

Rhinoceros

Kangaroo

Elephant

Hippopotamus

Giraffe

This page intentionally left blank.

Grassland Animal Patterns

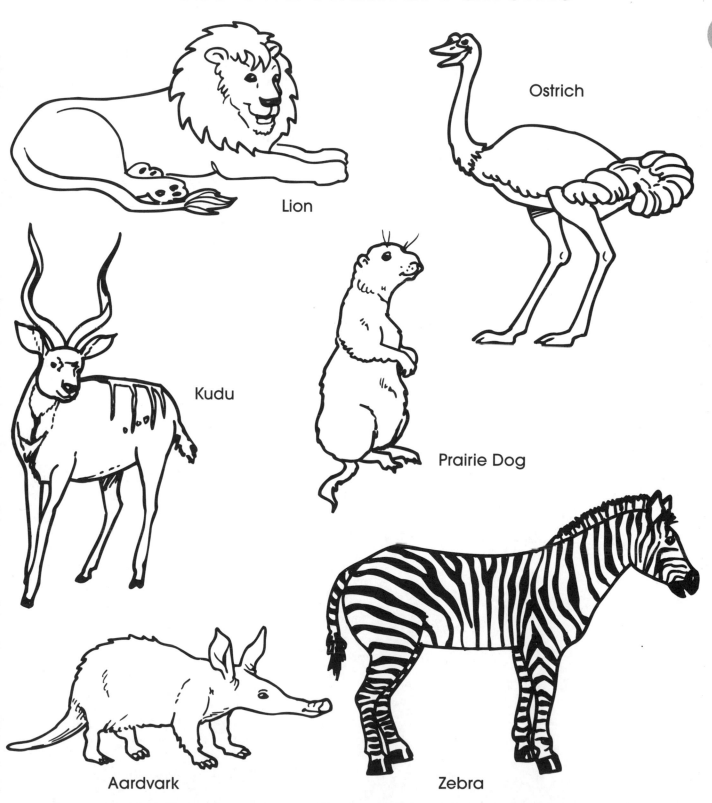

Lion

Ostrich

Kudu

Prairie Dog

Aardvark

Zebra

This page intentionally left blank.

At Home in the Grassland Community

Many animals make their homes in a grassland community, but some of the animals in this picture do not belong.

Directions: Draw an **X** on the animals that **do not** belong.

Life in a Rainforest

Share several books about the rainforest with your child and keep a running list of the animals that make their homes there. Give your child a piece of posterboard and a copy of the patterns on the next two pages. Tell him/her to color them, cut them out and glue them to the posterboard. Provide many visual aids so that your child can completely cover the posterboard with other rainforest animals and plants. He/she may paint or color his/her picture using many shades of green to illustrate the thick foliage. Discuss with your child the danger of extinction that rainforests face, and how we can conserve paper to prevent this!

Rainforest Animal Patterns

Howler Monkey

Toucan

Poison-Arrow
Frog

Iguana

Giant Anteater

Birdwing Butterfly

This page intentionally left blank.

Rainforest Animal Patterns

Macaw

Emerald
Tree Bag

Tamarin

Jaguar

Ring-Tailed
Lemur

Cock-of-the-Rock

This page intentionally left blank.

At Home in the Ocean Community

Many animals make their homes in an ocean community, but some of the animals in this picture do not belong.

Directions: Draw an **X** on the animals that **do not** belong.

Sea Animals

Explore the oceans and seas of the world with your young oceanographer to learn about the animal life they contain. Tell your child that the oceans and seas are home to many forms of plant and animal life. Your child may not realize that fish are not the only animals that live in the sea. Mammals, reptiles, mollusks and crustaceans also live there. Although not sea dwellers themselves, there are many aquatic birds that also depend on the animals of the sea for survival.

Examples of sea animals:

- Mammals: whales, seals, dolphins, walruses, porpoises
- Fish: sharks, sea horses, eels, rays
- Reptiles: sea turtles, leatherback turtles
- Mollusks: squid, octopuses, oysters, clams
- Crustaceans: shrimp, crabs, lobsters

Salt of the Earth

Do the following experiment with your child to demonstrate that salt water and fresh water differ in composition and that, therefore, most animals found in these types of water differ also. You will need two glass cake pans, a two-cup glass measuring cup, distilled water, salt, a spoon, two index cards and a pen. Pour one cup of distilled water into one glass cake pan. Pour a cup of distilled water into the two-cup glass measuring cup. Add salt to the cup of water until it won't dissolve any more. Then, pour it into the second cake pan. Label a card **Fresh Water** and place it with the first cake pan in a warm, sunny spot in your home. Label the second card **Salt Water** and place it with the pan of salt water next to the fresh water pan. Observe the cake pans the next day. Discuss the changes that occurred. When the water has evaporated from both pans, crusty salt will remain in one. Explain to your child that salt is the most common mineral found in sea water. However, sea water contains every mineral found on land. Point out that animals that live in salt water differ from animals that live in freshwater lakes and seas because their habitats differ.

Fun With the Food Chain

Discuss "food chains" with your child. Then, give him/her a copy of the pictures below and ask him/her to identify the pictures in the circles. Tell your child to cut out the

pictures and place them in an order to show who eats what. Next, give your child four 3" x 12" colored strips. Show him/her how to glue the two ends of one strip to make a link. Then, your child will slip the second strip through the first to form another link. Continue until the chain is complete. Finally, your child will glue one picture on each link in the correct order.

This page intentionally left blank.

Life in the Sea

Help your child to make a windsock using pictures of sea animals. You will need blue and green crepe paper strips, colored construction paper, one 2" x 18" tagboard strip, yarn, scissors, a hole punch, colored markers, glue and the sea animal patterns on page 145.

1. Staple the tagboard strip to form a circle.

2. Then, glue blue and green crepe paper strips in varying lengths to the inside of the circle. These represent the ocean waves.

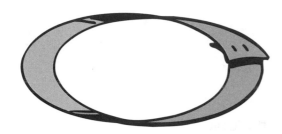

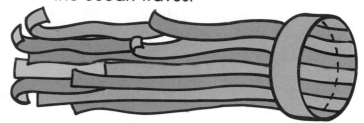

3. Next, color and cut out six or eight sea animals from construction paper using the patterns. Laminate these if the windsock will hang outside.

4. Trim the laminating film and staple the animals to the strips of crepe paper at different heights.

5. Finally, punch two holes opposite each other on the tagboard strip and tie a length of yarn from one to the other. The yarn can be tied together. Hang up the windsock.

This page intentionally left blank.

Sea Animal Patterns

This page intentionally left blank.

Section 4
Plants and Trees

Name_____

Parts of a Plant

Find a small plant to investigate.

Directions:

Describe your plant.
Then, draw a picture of each part.

The leaves are_____

_____

_____

_____ .

The stem is _____

_____

_____

_____ .

The roots are _____

_____

_____

_____ .

leaves
stem
roots

Plant Parts

A **plant** has many jobs. Each part has a special job.

Word Bank			
roots	stem	flower	leaf

Label the parts of the plant.

_____

_____

_____

_____

Draw a line from the
plant part to its job.

I make the seeds. ●
I make food for the plant. ●
I take water from the roots to the leaves. ●
I hold the plant in the ground. ●

Color the roots **red**.
Color the stem yellow.
Color the leaves green.
Color the flower **your favorite color**.

This page intentionally left blank.

Flower Fun

Directions:

Have your child write the words in the box below in ABC order on the petals. Then, he/she should cut out the petals and glue them on the circle to create a flower!

Word Bank
flower
vegetable
roots
petals
stem
leaf

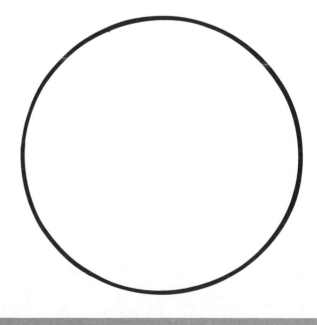

This page intentionally left blank.

Name_____

Animal or Plant?

All of the foods that we eat come from animals or plants.

Directions: Draw an **X** on the foods that **come from animals**.
Color all of the foods that **come from plants**.

carrot   egg   grapes

cheese   lettuce   chicken

banana   apple   fish

corn   ice cream   steak

Edible Plant Parts

We eat many plant parts. Sometimes we eat just the fruit.
Sometimes we eat just the leaves. We also might eat the stem,
the root or the seeds.

Directions:

Draw a line from the picture to the name of the plant part.
Color the plant part.

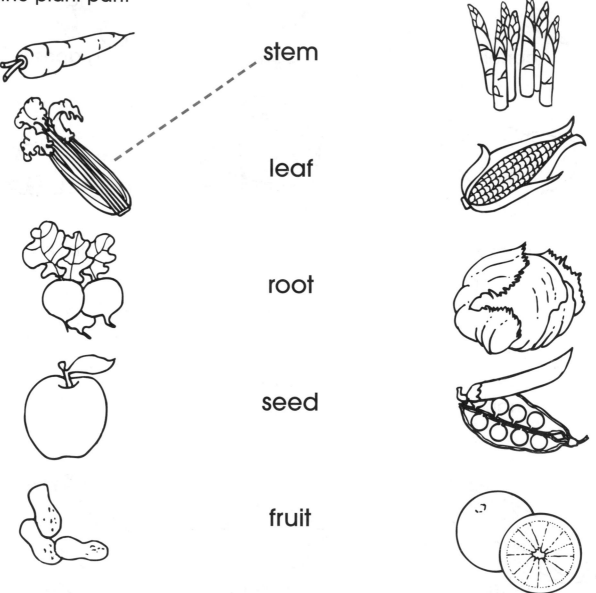

stem

leaf

root

seed

fruit

Growing Plants Flip Book

Directions: Color the pictures. Cut them out. Put the pictures in order on top of each other. (The youngest plant should be on top.) Staple the pictures together. Flip the pages and watch the plant grow!

This page intentionally left blank.

Name_____

Plant It Right!

Mr. Right and Mr. Wrong both planted gardens. Mr. Right planted his garden in the sun. Mr. Wrong planted his garden in the shade. Both of them gave their gardens love and care.

Draw what Mr. Right's garden will look like.

Draw what Mr. Wrong's garden will look like.

Name_____

Water, Please!

Mrs. Right planted her flower seeds last week. She planted them in the sun. She gave her flowers water.

Draw what Mrs. Right's flowers will look like.

Mrs. Wrong planted her flower seeds last week. She planted them in the sun. But she forgot to give them water.

Draw what Mrs. Wrong's flowers will look like.

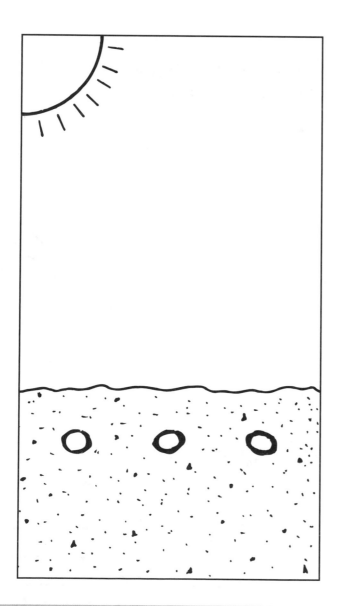

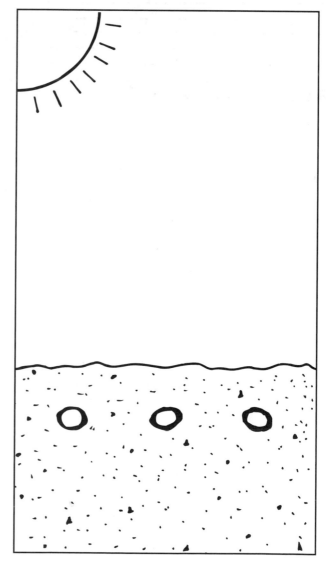

Growing Words

Directions: Write each word on the line below the correct picture.

pumpkin   seed   sprout   flower   plant

_____   _____

- - - - - - - - - - - - - - - -   - - - - - - - - - - - - - - - -

_____   _____

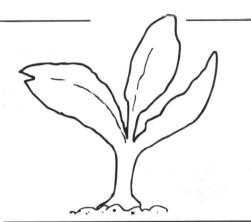

_____

- - - - - - - - - - - - - - - -

_____

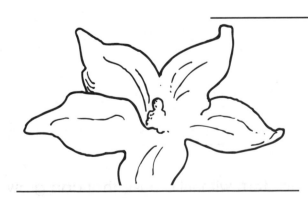

_____   _____

- - - - - - - - - - - - - - - -   - - - - - - - - - - - - - - - -

_____   _____

Eyes in the Dark

What has eyes, but cannot see? The potato! The little white bumps that grow on a potato's skin are called "eyes." An eye can grow into a new potato plant.

You will need:

potato
potting soil
flower pot or plastic glass

1. Put the potato in a dark cupboard or closet. Check it daily for small bumps called "eyes."

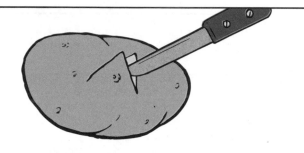

2. When the eyes appear, ask an adult to cut them off the potato.

3. Fill a flower pot half full of potting soil and lay the piece of potato on it with the "eyes" facing up.

4. Cover the "eyes" with 1 inch of soil. Water. Keep moist, but not wet. Watch closely for about two weeks.

What happened?

1 week

2 weeks

What happened?

A potato is a tuber. A **tuber** is a fat underground stem with little buds that can grow into new plants. The "eye" that you planted was really a potato bud that grew into a new plant.

Plant Puzzles

Help your child create plant puzzles to practice word and plant recognition! Color the pictures below. Cut out ten 3" x 6" cards from construction paper or tagboard. Glue one picture on the left side of each card. On the right side, write the name of the plant. You may want to laminate the cards and store them in an envelope. Cut each card in half so that the two pieces make a kind of puzzle. Be sure to use different cuts each time.

Have your child look carefully at each puzzle piece. He/she should match each plant picture with its name. For extra fun, ask your child to design new cards to add!

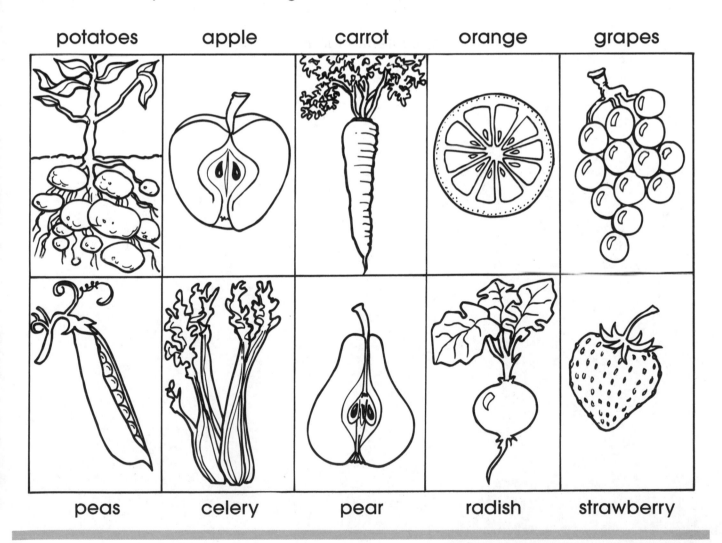

potatoes	apple	carrot	orange	grapes

peas	celery	pear	radish	strawberry

This page intentionally left blank.

Stems or Straws?

The **stem** of a plant carries water from the roots to the leaves. It is sort of like a **straw!** Try the experiment below to see this amazing feat!

EXPERIMENT

You will need two celery stalks with leaves. Cut off the bottom to create 6" stems. (White carnations also work, but the stems are not translucent!) You will also need two baby food jars or heavy cups, red and blue food coloring, water, masking tape, 2 spoons and a copy of the record sheet on the next page.

Directions:

1. Fill a jar or cup ¾ of the way with water.
2. Stir three drops of red food coloring in one jar and stir blue in the other.
3. Place a stalk of celery in each jar.
4. Check the stalks every hour and record the changes observed on the Record Sheet.

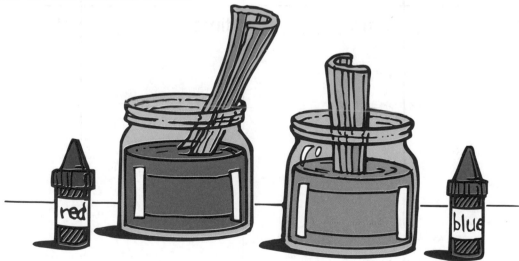

Name_____

Record Sheet

Observe your celery stalks every hour. Write and sketch your observations below.

	time _____	time _____	time _____	time _____
Red				
Blue	time _____	time _____	time _____	time _____

Name_____

Traveling Seeds

Seeds travel from one place to another. Sometimes people move the seeds. Sometimes they are moved in other ways.

Word Bank
people
animals
animals
wind
water

Finish the sentences to tell how seeds travel.

Seeds travel with _____ .

Seeds travel in _____ .

Seeds travel on _____ .

Seeds travel with _____ .

Seeds travel in the _____ .

How Many Seeds?

Plants have seeds. Some plants have one seed. Other plants have many seeds. When the seeds are planted, they grow into new plants.

Directions:

Write the name of the plant. Count the seeds and write the number of seeds beside the box. Draw a line from the seed to its plant.

_____
_ _ _ _ _ _ _ _ _
_____

_____ seeds

_____
_ _ _ _ _ _ _ _ _
_____

_____ seeds

_____
_ _ _ _ _ _ _ _ _
_____

_____ seed

_____
_ _ _ _ _ _ _ _ _
_____

_____ seeds

Tree Parts

Trees have three main parts: the trunk, the roots and the leaves. Each part has a special job. Each part helps the tree.

Directions: Cut out the name of each part. Cut out the job of each part. Glue them on the picture. Color the tree.

Name

Job

✂ —

| trunk | leaves | roots |

| I hold the tree in the ground. | I make food for the tree. | I hold most of the tree above the ground. |

This page intentionally left blank.

Name_____

From Acorn to Mighty Oak

Some trees drop their seeds in the spring.
Other trees drop their seeds in the fall.
The seeds grow up.
Do you know what they grow up to be?

Directions:

Show how the acorn grows into a mighty oak tree.
Write first, second or third under the pictures to put them
in order. Color the pictures.

_____ _____ _____

_____ _____ _____

Name_____

Trees Give Us Food

People eat many foods from trees. Animals can also eat the food from trees. The food comes from different parts of the tree.

Directions: Draw an **X** on the foods that **do not** come from trees. Label the foods that people get from trees.

Label the foods that animals get from trees.

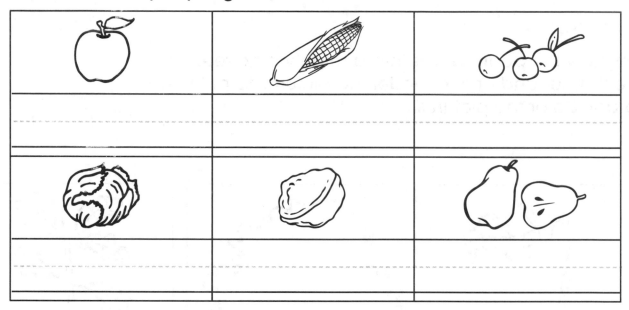

Word Bank
apple
corn
cherries
cabbage
nut
pear
acorn
carrot
bark
leaves

Name_____

Many Kinds of Trees

There are many kinds of trees. Each kind has a different name. Can you name some trees?

Circle the hidden trees.

```
O A K
A P P L E
P E C A N U L G H T
X Y O X S P R U C E
W A L N U T Z O M T
H B R W O R A N G E
C H E R R Y L E R X
B T R O L X P I N E
C E D A R H M T E R
```

Word Bank
oak
apple
cherry
pine
walnut
cedar
spruce
orange
pecan

Some of the trees above are fruit trees. Some are nut trees. Some are evergreen trees.

Write the tree names that belong in each list.

Fruit	Nut	Evergreen

I'm a Tree

Write the answer to each riddle in the puzzle.

Word Bank			
cherry	olive	lemon	rubber
ash	apple	maple	orange

Across:

4. I'm left over after a fire.
5. Part of me can be used to make bouncing balls.
6. My fruit is very sour.
7. I am either green or black.
8. People say George Washington chopped me down.

Down:

1. I make great syrup.
2. Many people drink my fruit's juice for breakfast.
3. Some say I keep the doctor away.

Maple Syrup Time

Spring is maple syrup time. People collect the sap from maple trees. They boil the sap until it becomes maple syrup. It takes thirty gallons of sap to make one gallon of syrup.

Directions:

Color the pictures. Write numbers next to the pictures in the order that maple syrup is made.

Trees Help Us

Trees are used in many ways. Sometimes we eat the food from trees. Sometimes we build things with the wood from trees. Can you name some things that come from trees?

Directions: Draw a line from the tree products to the tree. Circle the tree products.

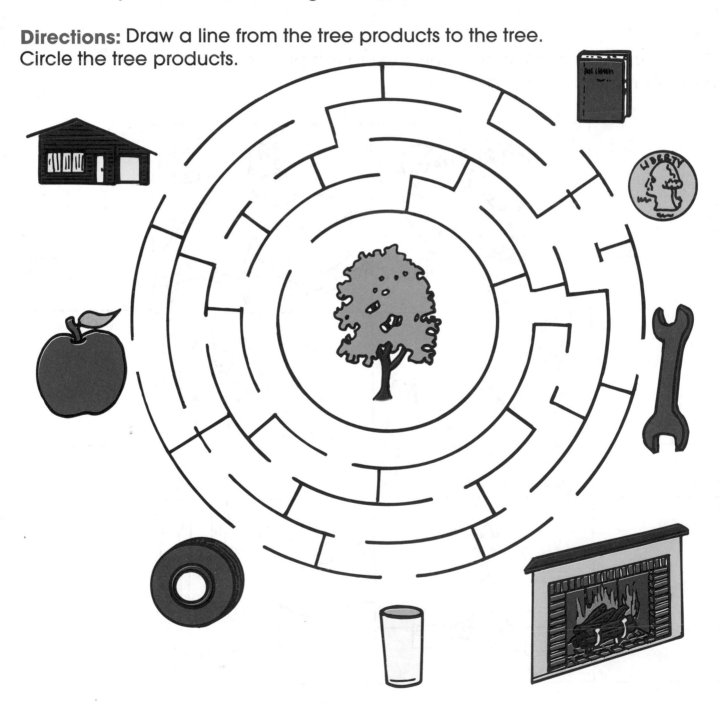

Name_____

Plant Puzzle

Use what you have learned about plants and trees to do this puzzle.

Word Bank
roots
seeds
trunk
sun
green

Across:

1. Plants and trees need light from the _____ to grow.

2. The _____ hold plants and trees in the ground.

4. Leaves must be _____ to make food for plants and trees.

Down:

1. Little _____ grow up to be plants and trees.

3. Most of the tree is held above the ground by the _____.

Looking at Leaves

This activity is best conducted in autumn in areas where trees lose their leaves in the fall. Leaves turn colors when the production of chlorophyll slows and finally stops. The red, orange and yellow pigments that were in the leaves when they sprouted begin to show around the edges and then replace the green pigment.

Help your child classify a variety of leaves according to different properties. Allow time to collect freshly fallen leaves. Draw the two intersecting circles of a Venn diagram (shown above) on a large sheet of paper for your child. Brainstorm categories he/she can use to classify the leaves. Possible categories include toothed and lobed edges, colors, textures and size.

lobed edges   **yellow**

lobed and yellow edges

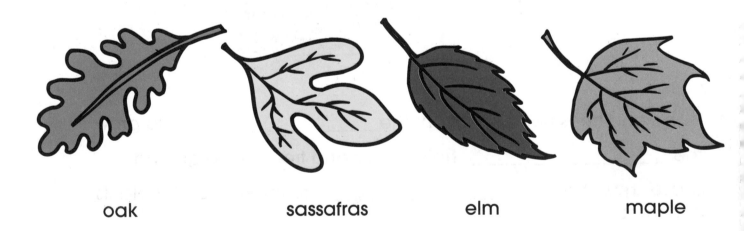

oak   sassafras   elm   maple

Leaf Study

Directions:

Put a leaf under this page. Rub the paper with the side of your crayon. Use a ruler to measure your leaf. Then, answer the questions below.

This is a rubbing of my leaf.

---

1. The color of my leaf is _____.

2. My leaf is _____ inches wide and _____ inches long.

3. My leaf feels like _____.

4. I found my leaf _____.

This page intentionally left blank.

Name_____

Parents: Provide more copies of this page so a booklet can be made.

My Leaf Collection

Attach a leaf and fill in the blanks.

Tree_____

Location_____

Date_____

This page intentionally left blank.

Parents: Provide more copies of this page so a booklet can be made.

My Leaf Collection

Attach a leaf and fill in the blanks.

Tree_____

Location_____

Date_____

This page intentionally left blank.

Food Factories

Green leaves are like little factories. They make food for the tree. Leaves need sunshine, air and water to make food.

Leaves change in the fall. They lose their green color. Then, they cannot make food for the tree.

Draw a leaf. This leaf can make food. Color it green.	Draw another leaf. This leaf cannot make food. Color it with pretty fall colors.

Directions:
Write the correct word.

_____

Food is made by _____ leaves.
          green   yellow

_____

Leaves need _____ to make food.
          shade   sunshine

_____

Leaves _____ make food in the fall.
     can   cannot

Those Lovely Leaves!

The leaves of plants have a very important job. They make the food for the entire plant. The leaves usually make food with a green substance found in them called chlorophyll. This is why most plants are green! Leaves can only make food, however, when they have enough sunshine and water. Try the experiment below to see the food that leaves make!

EXPERIMENT

1. Have your child rub a green leaf on paper. He/she will have to press hard.

2. Point out that what he/she sees on the paper is some of the plant's food.

3. Have your child follow the same procedure using several different leaves, both green and other colors. Have him/her predict whether or not the leaf will leave food on the paper first.

Extension: Have your child collect some of the following leaves: lettuce, cabbage, spinach, parsley, Brussels sprouts, Swiss chard, etc.

Cabbage

Brussels sprouts

Parsley

Swiss chard

Lettuce

Spinach

Leaf Poetry

Have your child follow the example below to write a cinquain poem about trees and leaves. Let your child copy his/her poem onto a large leaf pattern that matches the leaves written about in the poem.

Line 1: noun *Leaves*

Line 2: two adjectives *Lobed, golden,*

Line 3: three verbs with "ing" *Falling, twirling, blowing,*

Line 4: sentence *They change colors in autumn.*

Line 5: synonym *Pin oak.*

Haiku is a form of poetry made popular by the Japanese. It follows a pattern in which the first and third lines have five syllables, and the second line has seven. Haiku are usually written about nature.

The beautiful leaves,
Turning, twisting as they fall,
Flutter to the ground.

Section 5

Earth and Our Environment

Name_____

Our Planet Earth

Earth is the planet where we live. Earth has land and water. It gets light and heat from the sun. Earth has one moon. Earth is the only planet that we know has life. Many people think there is life on other planets. Do you think there is life on other planets?

Unscramble:

Earth is the _____ where we live.

l e t p n a
2 5 6 1 4 3

Check the sentences about the Earth that are true.

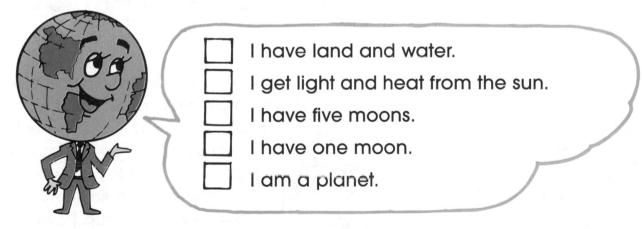

☐ I have land and water.
☐ I get light and heat from the sun.
☐ I have five moons.
☐ I have one moon.
☐ I am a planet.

Circle: Earth is the only planet that we know has

stars.

life.

Color: Draw one yellow moon in the picture.

Draw and color a picture of the Earth.

Taking Care of Our Home

Read the book *Just a Dream* by Chris Van Allsburg and discuss the problems with our environment that your child has noticed. Then, let your child try the experiments and activities below and on the next pages.

EXPERIMENT Landfill Pollution

Ask your child what he/she thinks happens to trash after it leaves your house. Explain to him/her that it is mashed and buried in a landfill. When rain comes along, the pollution from the trash is carried through the soil and may end up in a pond or river. Ask your child what this does to the soil and the water.

Have your child open a coffee filter and use markers to draw items on it that are normally found in your trash. Cover as much of the filter as possible. Next, use a pencil to punch holes in the bottom of a plastic cup. Slip the coffee filter into the cup. Have your child fill the cup with soil to "bury" the trash. Tell your child to now hold the cup over a tray and pour water over the soil (like rain). Watch as the water drips out of the cup. Ask your child what he/she notices. Ask what he/she thinks happens to the rain that washes through a landfill.

Taking Care of Our Home

Recycled Products

Explain to your child that he/she can help reduce the amount of trash that is buried by recycling paper, plastic and glass. When things are "recycled," this means that they are used again. Tell your child to watch for the recycling sign (to the left) on packages when you go shopping. Explain that this sign tells people that the package was made from recycled materials. Whenever you can, try to buy items with the recycling sign.

Have your child sort several empty packages according to recyclable and non-recyclable materials. Then, he/she can compare which items are better to buy and make a list to keep at home. You could also help your child graph the number of recyclable and non-recyclable items.

Paper Bag Fun

Tell your child that he/she can help the environment by using items again and again. For instance, take a cloth bag along with you when you go shopping. This way, you are saving paper bags and trees. Tell your child he/she could also save grocery bags.

Have your child decorate bags using recycling advertisements, and use them again the next time you shop.

Taking Care of Our Home

EXPERIMENT Save Water!

Families can also help keep our Earth healthy by conserving water. Tell your child that some people leave the water running in the bathroom sink when they brush their teeth. This wastes clean water! Try the activity below. Simulate a faucet running by pouring water from a jug into a bucket. Once water starts "running," have your child use a dry toothbrush to brush his/her teeth as normal. Keep pouring until he/she has finished brushing. Discuss how much water you "wasted."

Paper Conservation Rules

Discuss with your child ways to conserve paper:

- Always use both sides of a piece of paper.

- Always fill a paper from top to bottom.

- When you need a small scrap of paper, check your recycling container before using a new sheet.

I can just erase this mistake!

- Draw pictures in pencil and erase mistakes rather than starting over.

- Use the size of paper you need to do a good job rather than the largest piece available.

Recycling Center

Help your child sort items into groups of materials according to how they can be recycled. Keep the containers and have your child continue recycling.

METAL   GLASS   PAPER   PLASTIC   ALUMINUM

Recycling Center

Discuss with your child the importance of breathing in clean air. Explain to him/her that air pollution turns clear, odorless air into hazy, smelly air that harms health, kills plants and damages property. Brainstorm phrases your child could use on posters to encourage people and businesses to keep our air clean. ("Beware! We need clean air!" or "Oh, no! There's stinky air everywhere!")

Let your child illustrate the phrases on posterboard. Display them around your house, at your child's school and around town.

The Earth: Our Precious Fruit

To illustrate how little of our Earth can be used for food growth, do the following activity with your child.

1. Showing a whole apple, tell your child that this represents the Earth.

2. Slice the apple into quarters. Set aside three quarters for the oceans of the world, and one quarter for the Earth's land.

3. Slice the land quarter in half. Set aside one piece (uninhabited). Set aside another piece (inhabited).

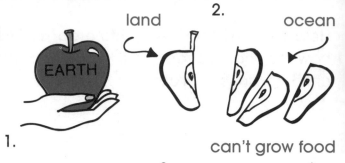

land   2.   ocean

1.

can't grow food

3.

4. Slice the "inhabited" piece into four equal pieces. Three pieces represent land too rocky, too wet, too steep or too crowded to grow food. One piece represents all the land we have left on which to grow food! ($\frac{1}{32}$ of Earth)

4.

land to grow food on

LAND

uninhabited   inhabited

Today and Tomorrow

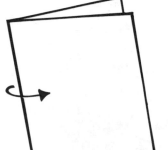

Look at several landscape pictures of Earth and discuss their beauty. Then, talk about how the landscape can change if we don't take care of our Earth. Fold a sheet of 12" x 18" construction paper in half to make two 9" x 12" pieces.

Open it and trace on the fold using a black crayon. Label one side **Today** and one side **Tomorrow**. Have your child draw the same landscape to illustrate today's beauty and tomorrow's possible destruction.

Today   **Tomorrow**

What You Can Do to Help!

Have your child make a plan of things
he/she can do to save the Earth.
Use the schedule below.

WE CAN SAVE
THE EARTH!

IDEAS	GOAL DATE	COMPLETED?	
		YES	NO
Start recycling at home.			
Turn off the water while you brush your teeth.			
Open the refrigerator only when it is necessary and close it quickly.			
Buy recycled containers and paper products.			
Take shorter showers or fill the tub with less water.			
Take your own bags to the store with you to use again.			
Switch to energy-saving fluorescent light bulbs.			
Use both sides of paper.			
Ride your bike or walk rather than asking for a ride in a car.			

This page intentionally left blank.

Name _____

Save, Save, Save Our Earth!

Sing the words below to the tune of
"Row, Row, Row Your Boat."

Save, save, save our Earth.
Keep it nice and green.
Reuse, recycle, reuse, recycle.
That'll keep it clean!

Try singing this in rounds!

• •

What Would You Do If . . .?

Role-play solutions to environmental problems.
Use the situations below as a starting point.

• You see someone litter on the street.

• Your mom leaves the water running in the kitchen sink.

• Your friend uses only half a piece of paper, then throws it away.

• Your brother picks flowers from a neighbor's garden.

• Your friend brings lunch to school every day, and always throws her lunch bag away.

What's Inside Our Earth?

EXPERIMENT

With your child, brainstorm ideas on what may be found deep inside the Earth. Then, share a poster or book illustrating the layers of rock and liquids that make up our planet. Because it took thousands of years to form these layers, tell your child that this experiment will take four days to complete.

Day One: Follow the directions to make a package of cherry gelatin and pour it in a pan. Explain that this represents the rocky center of the Earth. Refrigerate.

Day Two: Add a layer of orange gelatin. Tell your child that this represents hot liquid that can melt rocks. Refrigerate.

Day Three: Add a layer of lime gelatin with chopped fruit, and tell your child that this layer represents soil, mud and rocks that are closest to the Earth's surface. Refrigerate.

Day Four: Discuss the layers again and then eat them up!

Make a Volcano!

EXPERIMENT

Describe and discuss volcanoes with your child. Explain that they are proof of the liquid that is located deep in our Earth. Then let your child create a volcano. To do this, place a small jar in the center of a foil pan and shape a mountain around it using sand or mud. Be sure NOT to place sand or mud IN the jar!

Next, fill the jar ¾ full with vinegar. Then, add four drops of red food coloring to the vinegar and stir. Spoon small amounts of baking soda into the jar until it overflows creating a volcano!

Comparing and Classifying Rocks

Background Information for the Parent:

Rock is the solid matter which constitutes most of the Earth's crust. Rocks are very important objects of study because they are clues to the composition of the Earth, its age, history, geologic eruptions and so forth. Rocks are composed of minerals in varying amounts and combinations of incredible complexity.

Scientists classify rocks in many ways based on their mineral composition, structure, hardness, geographic location and many other factors. At your child's age, it is important to develop basic skills in comparison and classification, and rocks make an exciting and useful vehicle for developing these skills. Your child should use size, shape, color and degrees of roughness as initial areas of comparison. They can graduate to more complex methods of classification as they get older and more scientifically sophisticated.

Activity Suggestions for the Parent:

Review the instructions on the activity sheet on page 199 and set your child to work. Allow him/her freedom in the way he/she classifies. You will also want to be very flexible about how many piles he/she devises. The more complex your child becomes in his/her classifications, the more differences he/she will notice. Determining the relative hardness of rocks is a major means of classification for rocks. Your child could also arrange each rock in terms of its weight compared with its size.

This is also an opportunity to integrate math with science and to make measurements meaningful and vivid in your child's mind. Measure the length of the rock at its longest point and the width of the rock in inches. Each rock should be measured, described and labeled.

Name_____

Activity Sheet:
Comparing and Classifying Rocks

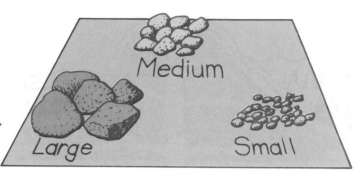

Medium

Large

Small

Directions:

Collect many different rocks.
Spread your rocks on top of a table.

Size:

Arrange your rocks in three piles by size.

Count the rocks in each pile.

Number of large rocks _____

Number of medium rocks_____

Number of small rocks _____

Color:

Arrange your rocks in three piles by color.

Count the rocks in each pile.

Number of dark-colored rocks _____

Number of medium-colored rocks _____

Number of light-colored rocks _____

List every color you see on these rocks. _____

_____

Feel:

Arrange your rocks in three piles by feel.

Count the rocks in each pile.

Number of smooth rocks _____

Number of rough rocks _____

Rockin' Into Rocks

Background Information for the Parent:

Rock is the solid part of the Earth's crust. Igneous, sedimentary and metamorphic are the three main kinds of rocks. Igneous rocks are formed when magma from deep inside Earth cools and hardens. Sedimentary rocks were formed when compressed layers of sand, mud, gravel or decayed plants and animals were deposited on the ocean floor millions of years ago. Metamorphic rocks are rocks that have been changed due to pressure, heat, liquids or gases. Rocks are made of different minerals.

Activity #1
Directions: Give your child an egg carton. Have him/her fill each compartment with a different kind of small rock. Encourage him/her to look in different places for the rocks or to dig for them. Display your child's collection on a table in your home.

Activity #2
Directions: Have your child choose a favorite rock from his/her collection. Have him/her tell: What makes it unique? Where was it found? Does it have a history? What kind of rock is it? Then, have your child draw a picture of his/her rock on a blank 5" x 7" file card.

Rockin' Into Rocks

Activity #3

Directions: With your child, brainstorm adjectives that relate to the size, shape, texture, color, luster, etc. of rocks. Write the adjectives on a chart to keep for other activities. Ask your child to write a short, descriptive paragraph about his/her favorite rock on a lined 5" x 7" file card. Staple it to the back of the file card with the rock's picture on it from Activity #2.

Who's an IGNEOUS?

Activity #4

Directions: Provide your child with ten or more rocks of different colors, shapes, sizes and textures. Give him/her a large sheet of butcher paper on which you have drawn a Venn diagram. First, ask your child to classify the rocks according to size. The large rocks should be placed in one circle, the small in the other and medium-sized circles should be placed where the circles intersect.

Then, have your child classify the rocks according to rough and smooth on the Venn diagram paper. Some rocks may have both rough and smooth parts and, therefore, should be placed in the center. Brainstorm other ways to classify the rocks, including by shape and color.

Finally, classify the rocks and see if your child can determine the criteria for the classification.

Rockin' Into Rocks

Activity #5

Directions: Give your child a ruler to lay the rock on to determine its length and width. Then, give your child a piece of string to measure the distance around the rock. Cut the string where it meets around the rock. Then lay the length of string on the ruler to find the circumference in inches.

Activity #6

Directions: To demonstrate how some rocks are changed, place two sandstone rocks on a piece of white paper. Have your child rub the two rocks together over the paper and observe the particles of sand that are rubbed off. Explain that wind and water can have the same wearing effect. If possible, show a smooth rock from a large lake or ocean. Explain that the force of the water crashing on the beach smoothed the rough edges of the rock over a long period of time.

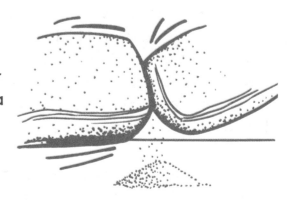

Next, show your child that limestone can easily be broken into smaller bits. Wrap a piece of limestone in a thick towel and tap it with a hammer to break it into smaller pieces. Observe the debris left from the break. Suggest that changes in the Earth's surface can cause rocks to break apart. Also, explain that roots from plants and trees are sometimes strong enough to break some kinds of rocks, and other rocks are broken by the freezing, thawing and refreezing of water in cracks in the rocks.

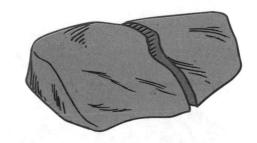

Rockin' Into Rocks

Activity #7

Directions: Let your child feel how heavy one ounce is. Then, ask him/her to select one rock from his/her egg-carton collection that he/she thinks weighs the same. Place a balance scale on a table and demonstrate how to use it correctly.

Have your child weigh each of his/her rocks, and categorize the rocks into sections of the egg carton according to "less than one ounce," "about an ounce" and "greater than one ounce." Use the balance scale and smaller weights to put the rocks in order from lightest to heaviest.

Activity #8

Directions: Have your child wash his/her rocks to remove foreign materials. Then, rub a rock firmly across the back of a piece of ceramic tile. Observe to see if a streak of color was left by the rock. Let your child try other rocks to see what colors are revealed.

Rocks With Lines

Background Information for the Parent:

There are three main groups of rocks: sedimentary, metamorphic and igneous. These groups are determined by the way the rocks are formed.

Igneous rocks are those which were once liquid. Rocks formed from lava fit into this group. Sedimentary rock is formed under oceans and seas. Sediment, composed of tiny bits of dirt, sand and organic material, settles to the floor of the ocean. The pressure of water over many years gradually presses this sediment into layers of rock.

Sedimentary rock holds the greatest store of fossils because of the way it is formed, and because oceans and seas often form over areas which were once above water.

Many fossils are so tiny, they cannot be seen. Others are as large as dinosaurs. Often sea shells or leaf patterns can be found in sedimentary rock.

Metamorphic rock is created when either igneous or sedimentary rock is subjected to great temperatures, pressure or hot water. Marble is an example of a metamorphic rock created from limestone, a sedimentary rock.

Activity Suggestions for the Parent:

You can buy decorative rocks at building supply stores. Some of these rocks will be sandstone or other common sedimentary rocks. Make sure some of the rocks have lines. You can also purchase rock specimens from science supply catalogs.

Explain to your child that he/she is looking for one kind of rocks—those with lines. A magnifying glass will help him/her count the lines and search for any fossils.

Name_____

Activity Sheet:
Rocks With Lines

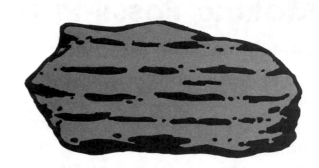

Directions:

Carefully look at each of your rocks with a magnifying glass.
Make a pile of all of the rocks which have lines.

How many rocks with lines do you have? _____

Choose one rock. Count the lines on the rock. How many

lines does it have? _____

What colors are on your rock? _____

Try This

Rub one of the rocks with lines.

How does it feel?_____

What came off when you rubbed? _____

Look

A fossil is an outline or part of a plant or animal which lived long ago.
Study each of your rocks with a magnifying glass. Did you find any fossils?

_____

Making Fossil Prints

Background Information for the Parent:

A fossil is an outline of the physical remains of an organism which lived long ago. The fossil is often mineralized or petrified by the action of water which seeped into the bone or wood of the organism. The water carried minerals which remained when the water evaporated. These minerals retained the impression of the organism. Many fossils are tracks, outlines or impressions of prehistoric creatures. A dinosaur track and the outline of a shell are examples of fossils.

Many fossils are found in sedimentary rock which was formed under the pressure of water. Tiny bits of sediment fell to the bottom of the ocean or sea and gradually formed rock containing many fossil specimens, especially of sea life.

This activity is designed to demonstrate to your child that an object in nature can form an impression. Clay is not sediment, of course, but when it surrounds an object, an impression is formed.

Activity Suggestions for the Parent:

Discuss the concept of a fossil with your child, and tell him/her that he/she is going to create his/her own fossil print.

Have your child find a few small objects in nature, and put them in the bottom of a plastic container. Have him/her press soft modeling clay over the objects at the bottom of the container and even it out so that the clay is at least $\frac{1}{2}$ to $\frac{3}{4}$ inch thick. Your child may want to roll the top of the clay flat and smooth with a pencil or crayon.

Leave the clay to harden overnight. The next day, use scissors to pry out one end or corner of the clay. You can also just cut away the container. Carefully peel out the clay and gently remove the objects. The print created by the objects is a fossil print.

Name_____

Activity Sheet: Making Fossil Prints

A fossil is an outline or a part of a plant or animal that lived long ago.

Making a Fossil Plant:

Gather several small objects found in nature like these:

shells	bark	leaves
dead insects	fish bones	feathers

Arrange these things in a box.
Some may overlap.
Work modeling clay with your hands until it is very soft.
Press the clay carefully into the box.
Cover the objects in the box. Leave the clay to harden.

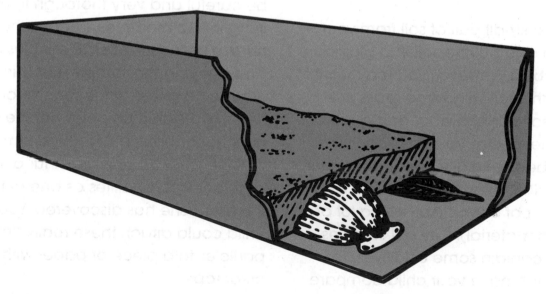

After the clay has hardened, turn your box upside down.
Pry the clay out with scissors.
Peel off the objects.
Trade fossil prints with a friend.
Guess what objects your friend has.

Soil Samples

Background Information for the Parent:

Soil is formed by the erosion of rocks through the action of wind and water. Soil will usually have small pebbles in it along with a good deal of decaying matter. Soil is enriched by the decaying organic material from plants and animals. The amount of organic material in a sample of soil will be determined by the location the soil was taken from. There is also some air and some water in a normal sampling of soil.

Activity Suggestions for the Parent:

Your child should be given a toothpick as a tool for separating the soil particles and a simple magnifying glass to study individual particles.

Dig up a small pail of soil from your garden and put the soil in a plastic cup or bag. However, you may want to enrich this soil with some grass cuttings, leaf parts, lawn or garden debris or whatever else you can find. This would be especially important if your soil is rather infertile or if you lack a rich layer of humus (soil with a lot of organic material). City soil samples should contain some additives. You could also have your child compare two samples, an enriched one and an unenriched one.

Stress to your child that he/she should be careful and very thorough in examining the soil samples. Require that he/she spend at least 20 minutes sifting and studying the sample. Encourage him/her to guess at the identity of types of organic particles he/she is uncertain about, and remind him/her that the smallest particle of fur or hair or spider web qualifies as one of the things he/she has discovered. Your child could attach these really tiny particles to a piece of paper with clear tape.

Activity Sheet: Soil Samples

Directions:

1. Spread your soil out on wax paper.

2. Make places for stones, plain soil and things which were once alive.

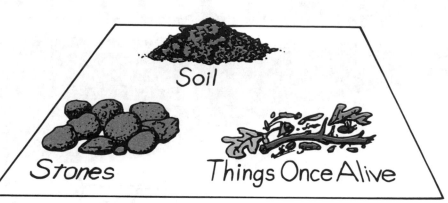

3. Use a toothpick to separate every bit of soil.

4. Use a magnifying glass to study every little bit of soil.

Circle the things you found:

leaf bits	worm	grass
paper bits	bone	spiderweb
root bits	bark bits	hair
insect part	fur	living insect

What was the most interesting thing you found? _____

What was the most surprising thing you found? _____

What do you think will happen to all of the things which were once alive?

_____

Water

Name_____

Sink or Float?

Why do some objects float? Why do other objects sink? Is it because of their shape? Is it because of their color? Let's find out!

You will need:
a large bowl of water
test objects, such as:
apple, nail, orange,
eraser, wood, stone,
egg, penny, crayon

Sinker or Floater?

1. List your objects.
2. Make predictions. Will they sink or float?
3. Test your objects to find the results.

Object	Prediction	Results

What happened?
If an object is heavy for its size, it will sink. If it is light for its size, it will float. A brick is heavy for its size, so it will sink. A piece of wood the same size will float.

Cohesion

Activity #1

Directions: Give your child a plastic straw and a sheet of wax paper. Place a spoonful of cornstarch in the center of the wax paper. Have your child predict what will happen to the cornstarch when he/she gently blows through the straw. (The cornstarch will blow away.) Then, have your child blow at the cornstarch.

Next, instruct him/her to predict what will happen if he/she blows at a drop of water through a straw. Using an eyedropper, place a drop of water on the wax paper. Have your child describe the shape of the droplet. (It is shaped like half a sphere.) Ask your child to gently blow at the water droplet. (He/she can move the whole drop of water because it holds together.) Explain that when the molecules of water cling together to form a drop, this is called cohesion.

Extension:
Provide your child with different colors of tempera paint. Have your child blow drops of the paint across colored construction paper to make free-form designs.

Cohesion

Activity #2
Directions:
Add red food coloring to water in a cup. Make a second cup of water blue. Give your child one piece of wax paper and two paper clips.

Ask your child to predict what will happen to a drop of water if he/she tries to move it from one side of a piece of paper to the other. Put one red drop of water on one edge of the wax paper. Put a blue drop on the other end. Explain to your child that he/she should try to move the droplets to the opposite sides of the wax paper using the paper clip.

Extension:
Have your child observe what happens if he/she stretches the droplet with the paper clip. (It can be stretched and will divide at some point. If that happens, he/she will be able to reunite the two parts.) Have your child merge the two droplets to see what happens when he/she tries to move a larger drop of water. (It moves more slowly.)

Surface Tension of Water: Overfilling the Cup

Background Information for the Parent:

Molecules of water have a tendency to adhere to each other. They are attracted to each other and pull toward each other in every direction. This molecular attraction allows substances to be buoyant, or to float on or in water. The attraction is particularly strong on the surface of the water because the molecules there have nothing above them to be attracted to and so they pull harder to the sides. This pulling creates a "skin" on the surface of the water.

This skin, caused by surface tension, is so strong that a container can be overfilled with water and still not spill. Instead of spilling over, the excess water forms a bubble above the container. In a plastic cup, this bubble can sometimes be ½ inch or so above the top of the cup. The bubble is very fragile and the water will spill if it is disturbed or if the surface tension is broken by a substance such as alcohol or soap. Alcohol and soap each reduce the attraction of these water molecules.

Activity Suggestions for the Parent:

Your child will enjoy doing the first activity and should try it several times. He/she may count as many as 50 eyedroppers full of water added to the cup after it was actually full. But make sure the cup is full before he/she begins counting. Your child will quickly realize that steady hands and careful attention will allow him/her to add more water than if he/she is careless and disturbs the water or the container.

The second activity can be done with many substances. You could use popcorn kernels, lima beans, other bean seeds, dried peas or aquarium gravel. Later in the activity, allow your child to use his/her own ideas for substances to add to the water.

Your child will be amazed at how many objects he/she can place in a full cup of water without spilling if he/she is very careful. Encourage your child to share techniques for placing the material in the water. Draw closure by reviewing the main concepts relating to surface tension.

Activity Sheet: Overfilling the Cup

You will need two cups of water. Fill one cup to the very top. Use an eyedropper to carefully add water to the full cup. How many eyedroppers full of water did you get into the cup before the water spilled?

_____

Fill the cup to the very top and try again. This time, how many eyedroppers full of water did you get into the cup before the water spilled?

_____

Try This

Fill the cup level to the top with water. Carefully place marbles in the full cup. How many marbles did you get into the cup before the water spilled?

_____

Try again.
How many did you
get into the cup this time?

_____

Paper Clip Boats

Background Information for the Parent:

This activity is a development of the previous lesson. The paper clip boats reinforce the concept that molecules of water tend to adhere to one another and that this attraction helps objects float. Surface tension, the "skin" on the surface of the water created by water molecules pulling to the sides, is strong enough even for some insects to walk upon.

An object which takes advantage of this surface tension can float easily. The aluminum foil covering the paper clip spreads the light weight over a wide surface, and the clip floats easily. Objects which are lighter than water compared to their volume can float.

A sheet of steel, for example, will not float. A steel ship, however, will float because the relative density of the ship is less than water due to the air which occupies so much space on the ship. (Density is the weight compared to the volume.)

Certain liquids, such as soap and alcohol, can reduce the surface tension of water by reducing the attraction of the molecules toward each other. When these are added to the water near an object, the stronger molecular attraction on the other side pulls the object forward.

Activity Suggestions for the Parent:

Give your child a plastic cup about $\frac{3}{4}$ full of water, a paper clip and a small piece of aluminum foil approximately two inches square. Your child will also need an eyedropper and a cup containing one inch or more of rubbing alcohol or dish soap.

Instruct your child to wrap the paper clip with the aluminum foil and to set this paper clip "boat" on the water so it will float. Show him/her how to place one drop of alcohol or dish soap in the water at the rear of the boat. The boat will shoot

forward because the surface tension at the rear is reduced, and the stronger attraction to the front will pull the boat forward. Your child will get the same result wherever he/she puts the alcohol, whether at the front or side of the boat. Your child can make the boat turn in circles by placing drops of alcohol repeatedly near one side. If he/she switches sides, the boat will twirl in the opposite direction. Your child can then make his/her own boat design, and he/she may shape the clip and the foil piece in different designs or different sizes.

Name_____

Activity Sheet: Paper Clip Boats

Making Your Boat

Directions:

Wrap a small paper clip with a piece of aluminum foil. You have made a paper clip boat.

Place your boat in the cup of water.

Did it float?_____

Place a drop of rubbing alcohol at the rear of the boat.

What happened to the boat?_____

_____

Place a drop at the front of the boat.

What happened? _____

Try to make the boat turn in circles.

How did you do it? _____

_____

Alcohol Boats

Background Information for the Parent:

This activity is a reinforcement of the two previous lessons on the surface tension of water. Rubbing alcohol and dish soap are two substances which reduce the attraction water molecules have for each other. This attraction is especially strong on the surface of water. A reduction of the attraction at one point on the surface will result in a pulling from the opposite point. In this experiment, when alcohol is added to the notch at the rear of the boat, the boat shoots forward. (Alcohol is a bit more effective than dish soap, but both work.)

Activity Suggestions for the Parent:

The actual floating of the boat might be done outside, if weather permits, so that any spillage will simply evaporate.

Give your child a 1" x 3" piece of cardboard and a 3" x 3" piece of aluminum foil. Your child will need an eyedropper, scissors and a small cup holding some alcohol or dish soap. Scraps of construction paper are ideal for the details of the boats. Glue, tape or rubber cement will be needed to attach these details.

When the boat is finished, your child can take it to a container of water. A toddler's wading pool works especially well. Smaller plastic or metal pans will also work. A drop of alcohol placed in the notch at the rear of the boat will propel the boat a few inches forward. Your child should notice how far he/she can propel the boat on a drop and how many drops are needed to get the boat across the container.

When your child makes the second boat, he/she will discover that the two notches work rather like twin engines, giving greater propulsion. The shape of the notch will also affect the speed somewhat. Your child might want to put notches on the sides for turning the boat.

As a follow-up activity, you may wish to view books in the library which deal with boats and floating. This activity is also a good vehicle for a written language activity in which your child describes the construction and use of his/her boat. Your child may also be motivated to draw and design boats as an art activity after this hands-on experience.

Activity Sheet: Alcohol Boats

Making the Boat

Directions:

Cut a piece of cardboard into a shape like this.

Cover the cardboard with aluminum foil.

Add seats and other details.

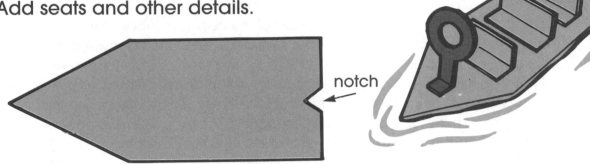

notch ←

Try This

Place the boat in the water.

Place one drop of alcohol in the notch.

What happened? _____

_____

Add another drop.

How many drops does it take to push the boat

across the container?_____

Try This

Make another boat.

Cut two notches in the rear.

Put a drop of alcohol in each notch.

What happened?_____

Capillary Action: Climbing Water

Background Information for the Parent:

Water has a tendency to "climb" into the very small spaces that are present in porous materials. This tendency is called capillarity. Capillarity accounts for the tendency of water to rise in plants and trees. It is applied in blotters and other substances used to soak up spilled liquids. In the soil, capillarity accounts for the tendency of water to climb through tiny spaces in the dirt and to evaporate at the surface, causing the soil to need irrigation of some type for crops to grow. In this experiment, the attraction between the molecules of water and the molecules of the paper goods causes the water to climb up the rolls of paper goods, against the force of gravity.

The tiny spaces in porous materials referred to above are like very thin tubes, or capillaries. Water tends to stick to the inside of these tubes and to climb. When the surface tension, or attraction between water molecules, is very strong, more water is pulled upward. The narrowness of the capillary tubes affects the speed of the climbing water; the narrower the tube, the faster the water will climb. Thus, in this experiment where three different paper goods are used, the tissue will usually be the first paper soaked since the weave of that paper is tighter and the tubes are narrower. Most paper towels will be the second soaked since their weave is a bit tighter than the napkin's weave.

Activity Suggestions for the Parent:

Show your child how to tightly roll the paper towels, tissues and napkins. Give your child a cup of water with a few drops of food coloring added to make the demonstration more dramatic. It is especially important to encourage your child to predict possible outcomes of the experiment before starting.

Tell your child to place the three paper rolls in the cups. Your child will quickly observe the climbing water during the investigation. The tissue, because of its tighter weave, will usually be the first paper soaked to the top. In the second part of the experiment, your child should tip the tops of the soaking rolls of paper into an empty cup, leaving the bottoms of the rolls in the colored water. The water will continue to climb the rolls until either the first cup is empty or the water is at

equal levels in both cups. If the rolls just touch over the lip of the second cup, instead of being tipped well into the second cup, the first cup will be emptied or nearly emptied. Be sure to have sponges or extra paper towels to clean up, as some water will drip onto the table. Doing the experiment outside would help you avoid this problem.

During your scientific discussion at the conclusion of the investigation, encourage your child to verbalize his/her conclusions and try to reinforce the main concepts. Ask your child to think of some real-life applications of the principle of capillarity. In addition to blotters, mops, sponges and other cleanup agents, your child may mention pens and some types of gauges.

Activity Sheet: Climbing Water

Directions:

Roll a paper towel, a tissue and a napkin. Place a few drops of food coloring in a cup of water.

What do you think will happen if you stand the rolls of paper in the cup of water?

_____

Do it.
What happened?

_____

Which roll of paper did the water climb first?

_____

Try This

What do you think will happen if you tip the tops of the

wet rolls into an empty cup?_____

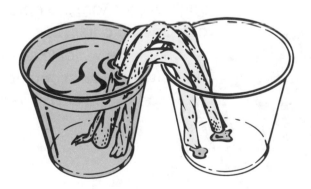

Do it.
What happened?_____

Water Displacement

Directions:

Pour food coloring into one cup of colored water in a two-cup glass measuring cup. Show your child a 2" diameter sandstone, limestone or shale rock. Ask him/her to predict what will happen if the rock is placed in the water. (It will sink.) Then, ask your child to predict what will happen to the water in the container. (The water will rise in the glass measuring cup.)

Using a marker, have your child draw a line on the activity sheet on page 223 to show the water level in the cup before adding the rock. Then, add the rock and have your child tell you how high the water is now. (It may have risen by a third of a cup.)

Explain that two things cannot occupy the same space at the same time. Because the density of the rock is heavier than the density of the water, the rock sinks. The water is displaced by an amount equal to the amount of space taken up by the rock. Your child can record the new water level on the chart by drawing a line and coloring up to it using a colored marker. Ask him/her to predict what will happen to the water level when the rock is removed. (It will fall back to almost the one cup level.)

Give your child an opportunity to test another object of choice. Ask him/her to mark the pictures on the activity sheet to reflect his/her findings. (Caution him/her to carefully remove each object from the colored water so that the water doesn't drip outside the cup. You may need to check the water level occasionally to make sure that the experiment always begins with exactly one cup of water.)

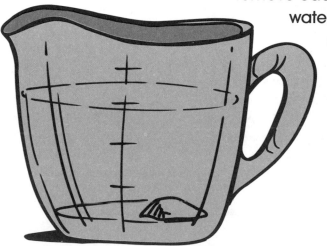

Activity Sheet: Water Displacement

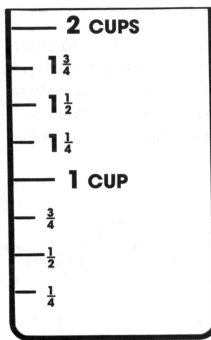

2 CUPS
$1\frac{3}{4}$
$1\frac{1}{2}$
$1\frac{1}{4}$
1 CUP
$\frac{3}{4}$
$\frac{1}{2}$
$\frac{1}{4}$

water level at start

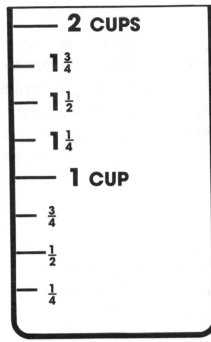

water level with rock

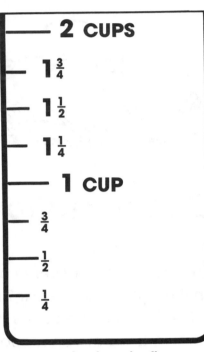

water level after
removal of rock

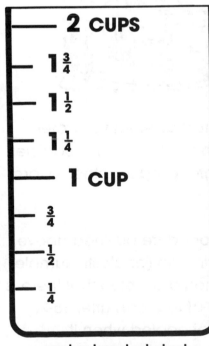

water level at start

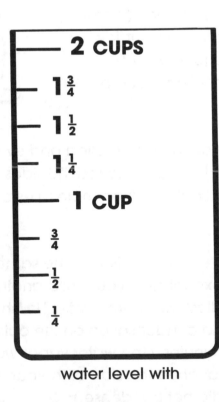

water level with
_____

water level after

removal of _____

The Water Cycle

Background Information for the Parent:
Water is the only element that is found naturally as a solid, a liquid and a gas. The waters of Earth go through a continuous cycle. They move from the oceans, to the air, to the land and back to the oceans by means of evaporation, condensation and precipitation.

Condensation

Directions:

Ask your child to observe a can. Is there any moisture on the outside of the can? (No.) Then, have your child fill the can with ice cubes and set it on a paper towel in a warm, sunny spot in the room. After 15–20 minutes, have your child look at the outside of the can. What has happened? (Water vapor in the air has condensed on the outside of the can. Some droplets have joined and trickled down the side of the can. The piece of paper towel is wet.)

Explain that some of the ice inside the can melted and evaporated. When the water vapor in the warmer air outside the can touched the sides of the cold can, the particles condensed and formed water droplets. When molecules of water cling together to form a drop, it is called cohesion.

Variation: Follow the same procedure outlined above, except give your child another tin can (or plastic tumbler) filled with warm water. He/she should observe that there is no condensation on the outside of that can after 15–20 minutes. (The water vapor was not cooled when it touched the side of the can of warm water. Therefore, it did not condense.)

Precipitation

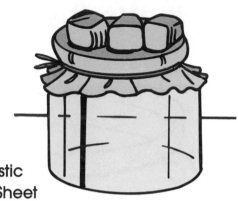

Directions:

Cover a work area with newspaper. Pour 1½ cups of warm water into a clean pint jar. Seal the top with a layer of clear plastic wrap. Be sure the top is taut and that the wrap adheres to the jar (Use a rubber band or string to secure.) Carefully place three or four ice cubes on the top of the plastic wrap. Have your child complete drawing **#1** on the Activity Sheet on page 226.

After 15 minutes, move the melting cubes onto a piece of paper towel. Do not remove the plastic wrap. There will be water from the melting cubes on the top of the wrap, but your child will still be able to observe that tiny water droplets formed on the underside of the plastic wrap. Some of the droplets have joined, becoming bigger drops. Have your child complete drawing **#2**. Have him/her predict what will happen next.

Your child should watch the surface of the water inside the jar. After a while, water drops will fall onto the surface. Have your child complete drawing **#3**. Explain that when water vapor that forms clouds is cooled, it condenses. The droplets combine and adhere to other small particles in the atmosphere like dust and smoke. When the droplets become heavy, they drop from the cloud in the form of precipitation. Precipitation can be in the form of rain, hail, sleet or snow, depending on the temperature.

Extension:

Teach your child about the different kinds of clouds. Explain to him/her that clouds are always changing shape because parts of them continue to evaporate when the cool air of the cloud meets warmer air. Wind can also affect the shape of clouds.

Activity Sheet: Precipitation

#1. Draw what the jar looks like now.
Time: _____

#2. Draw what the jar looks like now.
Time: _____

#3. Draw what the jar looks like now.
Time: _____

Draw a picture of your favorite
kind of precipitation.

Evaporation

Directions:

Remind your child that particles of water stick together. For example, many raindrops form a puddle. Take your child outside on a warm, sunny morning. Carry a bucket of water to a spot of pavement. Use an eyedropper to show one drop and then another building up on it, etc., until it is clear that the droplets stick together and begin to form a puddle. Then, add more water to make a small puddle in the sun. Have your child trace the outline of the puddle using a piece of sidewalk chalk. Note the time.

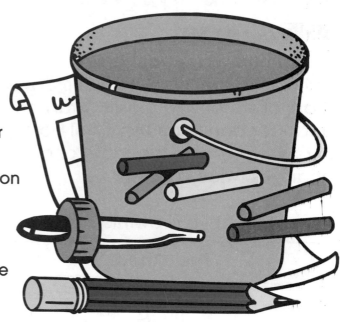

Return to the puddle in an hour. Have your child trace the outline of the puddle using a different color of chalk. Were there some changes? (The puddle should have shrunk a little.) Discuss what caused the change in the size of the puddle. (The warmth of the sun heats the water, causing it to turn into a gas. However, do let your child know that other factors, like wind, can accelerate evaporation.) Explain that this process is called evaporation. Continue to return until the puddle has evaporated.

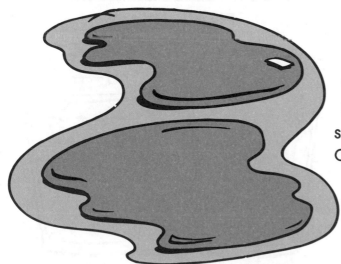

Variation:

Make another puddle in the shade at the same time you make a puddle in the sun. Compare the different rates of evaporation.

Where's the Water?

EXPERIMENT

Directions: Have your child fill two glasses halfway to the top with water. Cover one glass of water with plastic wrap and place a rubber band around it. Set both glasses in a warm spot in the room and check for changes twice a day.

Have your child draw his/her results below.

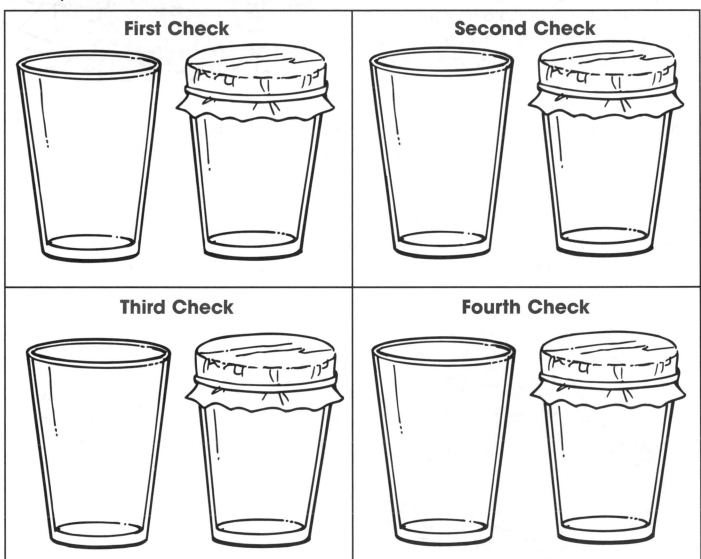

First Check

Second Check

Third Check

Fourth Check

Salty Water Evaporation

You will need:

spoon, salt
paper cup
$\frac{1}{4}$ cup water

Directions:

1. Stir the salt into water.

2. Put the cup in a warm place.

3. Predict: What do you think will happen to the water?

_____

What do you think will happen to the salt? _____

_____

4. Check the cup in a few days and record:

What has happened to the water? _____

_____

What has happened to the salt? _____

_____

Ice

Activity #1
Directions:
Measure one tablespoon of water into several one-ounce portion cups. Place them in a muffin pan, and put the muffin pan in the freezer. Note the time. Predict how long it will take for the water to turn into ice. Check every fifteen minutes. Record the time when the portion cups are frozen. Observe the portion cup to see that ice has more volume than water. (Keep the cubes frozen to use in Activity **#2** on page 231.)

Variations:
Freeze other liquids such as juice, soft drinks and milk in addition to water. Keep a graph showing the time it took to freeze each liquid. (Water freezes at 32°. It will freeze the fastest if all other conditions are the same with the other liquids.)

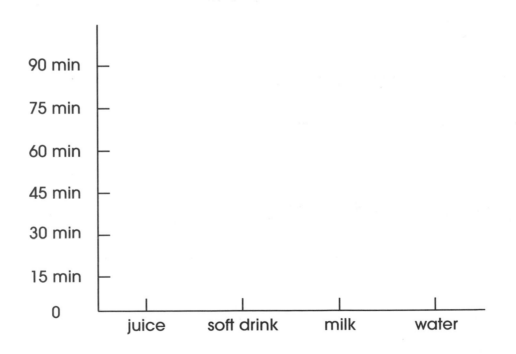

90 min			
75 min			
60 min			
45 min			
30 min			
15 min			
0	juice	soft drink	milk	water

Ice

Activity #2

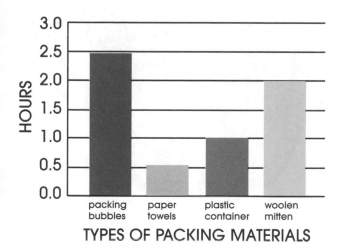

HOURS vs TYPES OF PACKING MATERIALS

- packing bubbles: ~2.5
- paper towels: ~0.5
- plastic container: ~1.0
- woolen mitten: ~2.0

TYPES OF PACKING MATERIALS

You will need:
graph paper
markers
6 pint-sized, resealable plastic bags
ice cubes in portion cups (from Activity #1)
the following items to be used as insulators:
packing bubbles, paper towels, small plastic
container with an airtight lid, a cup of
shortening, pencil shavings, a woolen mitten

Directions:
Explain to your child that he/she will try to keep one ice cube from melting.
Have him/her select one packing material for the ice cube and a resealable
plastic bag. He/she should decide how best to use the packing material to
insulate an ice cube in the resealable plastic bag. Remove the portion cups
from the freezer and give an ice cube to your child. Note the time. Your child
should work rapidly to insulate the ice cube and seal it in the plastic bag. Check
the ice cube every half hour. Note the time the cube melted.

Allow your child to experiment with other insulators. Discuss
theories about why some things were better
insulators than others. Talk about what
things are used as insulators to keep ice
from returning to a liquid state. (Note:
There will not be a tablespoon of water
left in the bags after the ice cube melts.
This is because the property of adhesion
makes the water molecules adhere to
some of the packing materials.) Make a
bar graph showing the time each ice
cube melted.

Fish Float

You will need:

2 two-cup glass measuring cups
distilled water
salt
tablespoon
spoon
2 fresh eggs

Directions:

1. Pour one cup of distilled water into one two-cup measuring cup and carefully lower a "fish" (a fresh egg) into it. (The egg sinks near the bottom. None of the egg is showing above the water.)

2. In the second cup, stir in two tablespoons of salt until dissolved. Ask your child to predict what will happen when a fresh egg is lowered into the salt water.

3. Add the egg to the salt water. (The egg floats with part of the top showing above the water. Ask your child to predict what will happen if another tablespoon of salt is added to the water.

4. Remove the egg, add the salt and stir until dissolved.

5. Then, replace the egg. (The egg will float higher in the saltier water.) Discuss with your child that the density of salt water helps support large fish like 1,500-pound sharks and huge mammals like two-ton whales.

Water Wizard Game

Background for the Parent: Water has three forms: solid (ice), liquid and gas (water vapor). Cohesion and adhesion are characteristics of water. About three-fourths of the Earth is covered with water. Of that, about 97% is salt water. All living things need water. The water on Earth today is the same water that was here millions of years ago.

You will need: one copy of the spinner and token patterns (below), one copy of the Water Wizard pattern (page 235), one copy of the gameboard (pages 237 and 239), file folder, glue, brass fastener, plastic lid, safety pin or paper clip, scissors, crayons, markers, laminating film

token

token

Directions:

1. Color, cut out and glue the Water Wizard onto the front of a file folder.
2. Color, cut out and glue the two gameboard pages to the inside of the file folder.
3. Cut out the spinner, laminate it and glue it to a plastic lid. Put a brass fastener through a paper clip or safety pin and then through the center of the lid.
4. Color each token a different color. Cut them out and laminate them.

Three Forms of Water Spinner

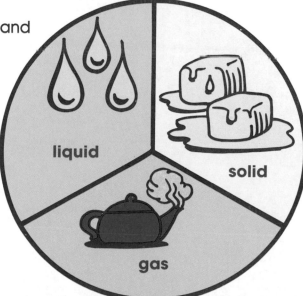

Directions for Two Players:
Each player chooses a token and places it on START. Player 1 spins the spinner and moves to the first space that matches the picture (form of water) on the spinner. He/she does what is indicated in the space. Players take turns spinning. The first player to reach FINISH is the Water Wizard!

This page intentionally left blank.

Name_____

Water Wizard Pattern

This page intentionally left blank.

Water Wizard Gameboard

This page intentionally left blank.

Water Wizard Gameboard

This page intentionally left blank.

Water Writing

Show your child how to write an acrostic poem about water on a raindrop shape.

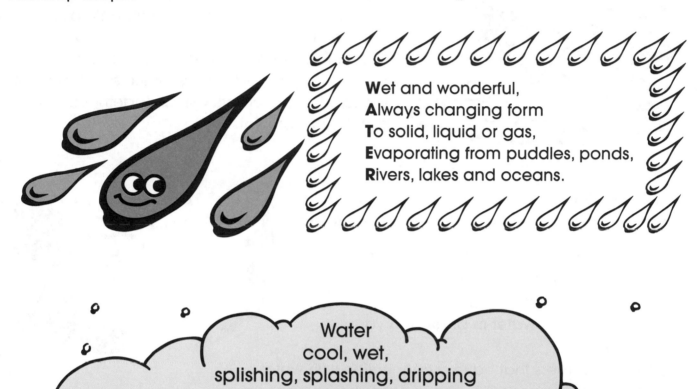

Wet and wonderful,
Always changing form
To solid, liquid or gas,
Evaporating from puddles, ponds,
Rivers, lakes and oceans.

Water
cool, wet,
splishing, splashing, dripping
cold, frozen
Ice

Writing a diamante poem is an excellent way to reinforce the concept that water has different forms. The poem can show the change from a liquid to a solid, as in the example above, or from a liquid to a gas, or the reverse of these. Print the poem on a watercolor wash. (See the Art Suggestion on page 242.)

Your child can write a paragraph using one of the topic sentences below.

• If I were a form of water, I'd want to be a (solid, liquid, gas) for two reasons. . . .

• If I were the Water Wizard, I'd change all the water on Earth into. . . .

Water Extension Activities

Art

Your child can make a watercolor wash to use as a background for his/her diamante poem. Using a clean, wet sponge, dampen a 9" x 12" sheet of white drawing paper. Use a large paintbrush to apply watercolors. Make sure the paint is diluted so the colors will run together on the paper. Let it dry flat.

Social Studies

Try one or all of the activities below with your child:

- Outline the oceans on a large wall map.
- On an outline map of the world, color land areas green and water areas blue.
- Discuss sources of water in or around your community.
- Brainstorm careers that have a connection with water (i.e., oceanographer, sailor, river boat or barge captain, swim instructor, lifeguard, diver, water theme park worker, member of the United States Navy or Coast Guard, etc.).

Award

After completing the water activities, allow your child to color and cut out the Water Wizard badge and wear it.

Section 8
Weather and Seasons

Weather Watch

Weather is the condition of the air around the Earth for a period of time. A weather forecaster's job is to predict the weather.

There were some very unusual weather patterns recorded for a recent month. Use the key to draw the correct weather symbols for each day.

- Every Monday and Tuesday it rained.
  Then, it was sunny for the following three days.

- On the first and third weekends, the first day was cloudy, and the second day was snowy.

- On the second and fourth weekends, it was just the opposite.

Key

sunny

cloudy

rainy

snowy

Sun.	Mon.	Tue.	Wed.	Thurs.	Fri.	Sat.
		1	2	3	4	5
6	7	8	9	10	11	12
13	14	15	16	17	18	19
20	21	22	23	24	25	26
27	28	29	30	31		

Write the word that tells about the weather on these dates:

- 6th day of the month _____
- 13th day of the month _____
- last day of the month _____

Name_____

Sky Watch

Weather changes often. Will tomorrow's weather be like today's? Keep a weather chart for one week to find out!

Directions: Record the weather in the morning and afternoon by drawing the correct pictures on the chart below.

| rainy | snowy | sunny | cloudy | partly cloudy |

This Week's Weather				
	Monday	**Tuesday**	**Wednesday**	**Thursday**	**Friday**
A.M.					
P.M.					

This page intentionally left blank.

Name_____

Hot or Cold?

A thermometer tells us the temperature. Make your own thermometer and practice reading the temperature.

Directions:

1. Color the bottom half of the tube **red**.

2. Cut out the tube.

3. Cut the slits **A** and **B** on the thermometer.

4. Fold and insert the ends of the tube in slits **A** and **B**.

5. Slide the tube up or down and read the different temperatures.

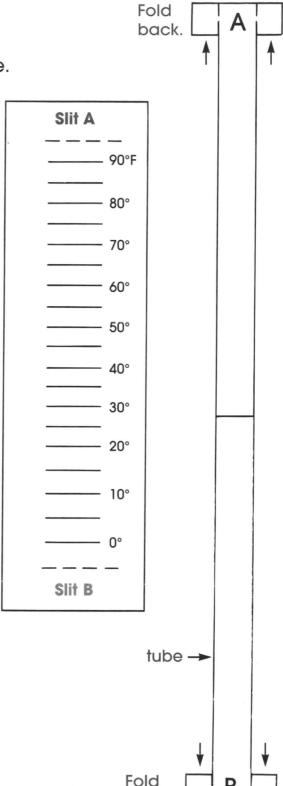

Fold back. A

Slit A

— 90°F

— 80°

— 70°

— 60°

— 50°

— 40°

— 30°

— 20°

— 10°

— 0°

Slit B

tube →

Fold back. B

This page intentionally left blank.

Name_____

A Nice Day Outside

It is nice to play outside on hot days, cold days and mild days. Look at the temperature in each picture. Write the temperature and **hot**, **cold** or **mild** to tell what kind of day it is.

Our Changing Weather

As your child starts dressing differently for a new season, he/she will become more aware of the changing temperature.

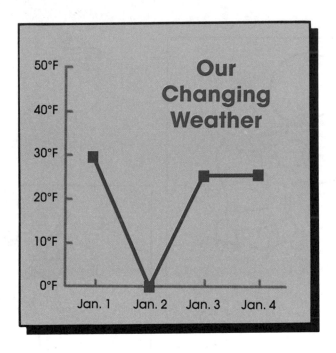

Directions:

1. Use a piece of butcher paper to create a graph as shown. Label the bottom with dates and the side with temperatures.

2. Put a thermometer in a shaded area outside your home.

3. Send your child to check the temperature at the same time each day.

4. When he/she returns, record the daily temperature with a dot and connect it with the previous day's temperature to emphasize changes.

Be a Weather Reporter

Directions:
Using the form below, have your child give a weather report each morning at breakfast time.

Today would be a good day to stay inside!

And Now . . . Today's Weather!

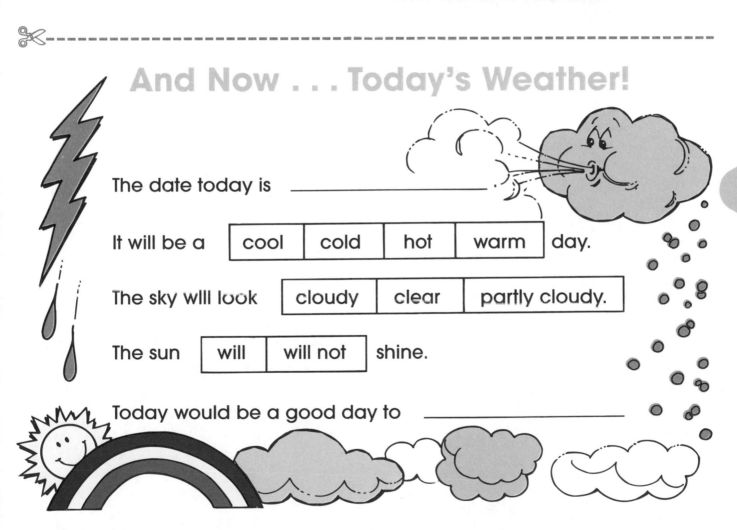

The date today is _____

It will be a | cool | cold | hot | warm | day.

The sky will look | cloudy | clear | partly cloudy.

The sun | will | will not | shine.

Today would be a good day to _____

This page intentionally left blank.

Weather Dominoes

Preparation:

Cut twenty-four 3" x 6" "dominoes" out of cardboard or construction paper. Draw a black line through the center of each. Glue one of the weather pictures (below and on the next page) to one end of each domino. Then, write a weather word on the other end of the domino. Laminate the dominoes and put them in an envelope for storage.

Directions:

1. Shuffle the dominoes and spread them out face-down.
2. Each player chooses seven dominoes to begin but keeps them hidden.
3. The first player lays a domino down, and the next player matches it, if possible. If not, he/she draws from the stack. The first player to run out of dominoes is the winner!

This page intentionally left blank.

Name_____

Weather Dominoes

This page intentionally left blank.

Make a Rainbow!

EXPERIMENT

Directions:

1. On a sunny day, fill a large glass bowl halfway with water.

2. Next, set a mirror in the water.

3. Have your child move the mirror until a rainbow is formed on the walls of the room.

4. Tell him/her to let the water settle to make the rainbow more clear. Have your child color the rainbow below to show what he/she saw.

What Happened?
Rainbows are formed when light is bent, releasing all the colors of the rainbow. The water bends the sunlight, forming a rainbow.

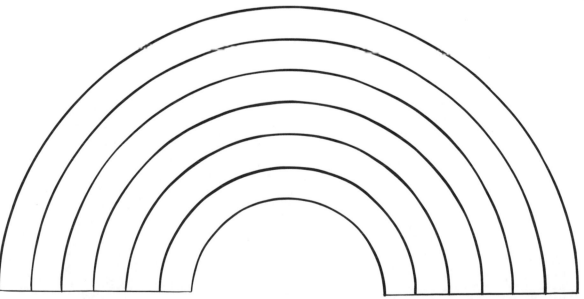

Rainbow Toast

You will need:

1 cup of milk
4 slices of white bread
4 tablespoons of sugar
4 plastic cups
4 new paintbrushes
4 colors of food coloring
foil
toaster oven or broiler

Preparation:

Fill each of the four cups with $\frac{1}{4}$ cup of milk.
Use food coloring to make each cup a different color.

Directions:

1. Instruct your child to use the paintbrush and colored milk to paint a rainbow on two slices of bread laid out on the foil.
2. Sprinkle sugar on top.
3. Toast the bread until it is slightly brown.
4. Enjoy!

It's Raining Cats and Dogs!

Directions:

Discuss the expression "It's raining cats and dogs!" as it relates to heavy rain. Talk about how funny this would look, and the strange places the animals would land! Then, try to think of some other silly types of "rain" and illustrate together. Your child can then choose his/her own creative rainfall, write the expression on paper and illustrate it. Enjoy *Cloudy with a Chance of Meatballs* by Judith Barrett (Atheneum Press).

The Rain on the Roof
(sing to the tune of "The Wheels on the Bus")

Let your child sing these verses and then let him/her make up some new verses to try!

The rain on the roof goes pitter, patter, pit; pitter, patter, pit; pitter, patter, pit.
The rain on the roof goes pitter, patter, pit, all through the storm.

The lightning in the sky goes flash, flish, flash; flash, flish, flash; flash, flish, flash.
The lightning in the sky goes flash, flish, flash; all through the storm.

The thunder from the clouds goes boom, bang, boom; boom, bang, boom;
*   boom, bang, boom.*
The thunder from the clouds goes boom, bang, boom; all through the storm.

Let your child try finishing these verses that describe a rainy day:

The drops in the puddle . . .
The flowers in the garden . . .
The kids stuck inside . . .
The sun comes along and . . .

The Perfect Raincoat!

EXPERIMENT

Directions:

Prepare a 2" x 10" piece of the following materials: foil, plastic wrap, tissue, cloth, paper and newspaper. Have your child predict which material will keep a pencil dry when it is dipped in water. Have your child record his/her predictions on page 261. Then, have him/her wrap a pencil tightly in each of the 2" x 10" pieces of material and dip it in water for five seconds. Unwrap and check the pencil to see which materials kept it dry. Your child should record his/her results on page 261.

The Perfect Raincoat!

EXPERIMENT

Directions: Color the raincoats you think will be the best.
Draw an **X** over the raincoats you think won't work at all.

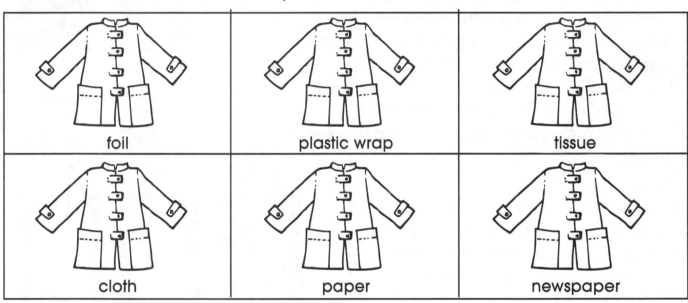

foil | plastic wrap | tissue

cloth | paper | newspaper

Directions: Color the raincoats that worked the best.
Draw an **X** over the raincoats that didn't work at all!

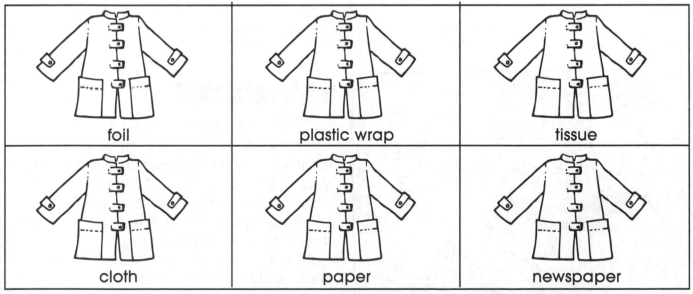

foil | plastic wrap | tissue

cloth | paper | newspaper

Can you guess which material is used to make many raincoats?

_____

Make a Cloud

E X P E R I M E N T

Directions:

1. Have your child fill a 2-liter plastic bottle container $\frac{1}{3}$ of the way with warm water.
2. Tape black paper to the back of the container.
3. Light a match and drop it in the container.
4. Let your child help you immediately cover the container with a small plastic bag of ice.
5. Watch for a cloud. The paper will help you see it!

What Happened?

Clouds form as warm water evaporates and forms drops on small pieces of dust in the air (match smoke). This happens in the sky where the atmosphere is cool (ice).

Cotton Clouds

E X P E R I M E N T

Directions: Read *The Cloud Book* by Tomie de Paola. Then, discuss the characteristics of different clouds. Provide your child with a 9" x 12" sheet of blue construction paper and 6-7 cotton balls. Let him/her use the cotton balls to create three types of clouds, using the book as a guide. Then, he/she can use crayons to finish and title the picture.

Make It Rain in Your House!

EXPERIMENT

Directions:

1. Boil water until steam rises (evaporates).

2. Hold a tray of ice about five inches above the steam. Put a pan or tray underneath to catch the "rain." Be careful to keep your hands and arms away from the steam.

3. Continue holding the tray until drops of water form on the bottom of the tray, grow heavy and fall like rain!

What Happened?
The water evaporates (steam) and collects where the air is cool (ice). As more water evaporates, the drops bond to form larger drops that eventually fall to the ground.

Name_____

The Water Cycle

All of the water on Earth travels on a never-ending journey. This journey is called the water cycle. There are three steps to the water cycle: **precipitation**, **evaporation** and **condensation**.

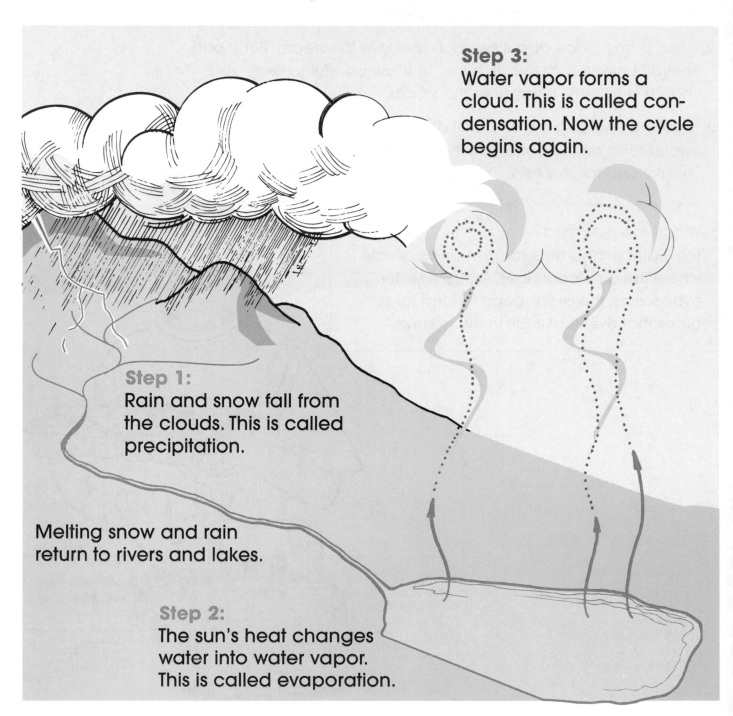

Step 3:
Water vapor forms a cloud. This is called condensation. Now the cycle begins again.

Step 1:
Rain and snow fall from the clouds. This is called precipitation.

Melting snow and rain return to rivers and lakes.

Step 2:
The sun's heat changes water into water vapor. This is called evaporation.

How Are Clouds Made?

Directions:

Cut out the pictures.
Glue them on the page to
show the water cycle.

This page intentionally left blank.

Cloudy Weather

Clouds bring us many kinds of weather. Some clouds give us fair weather. Other clouds bring rain. Glue the picture of the cloud next to its description.

	How the Clouds Look	Weather
	Big, puffy clouds that look like cotton.	Nice day, but there might be a small shower.
	Tall, dark piles of clouds that are flat on the bottom.	Thunderstorms likely.
	Wispy clouds that look like feathers.	Fair and sunny.
	Layers of gray clouds that cover the whole sky.	Steady drizzle.

Cloud Cake

You will need:

20 chocolate wafer cookies
8 oz. whipped cream
plastic knife
plastic fork
paper plates

Directions:

1. Instruct your child to spread the top and bottom of the cookies with whipped cream.

2. Stand the cookies on their sides and press them together to create a long row.

3. Have your child cover the entire roll with whipped cream.

4. Refrigerate the entire dessert for two hours. Then, eat up!

Make a Tornado in a Jar!

EXPERIMENT

Directions:

1. Have your child fill a jar with water.
2. Next, add salt and a very small drop of liquid soap from the tip of a toothpick.
3. Have him/her tighten the lid on the jar.
4. Instruct your child to turn the jar sideways and hold the lid in his/her left hand and the bottom of the jar in his/her right hand.
5. Have your child rotate the jar vigorously for several seconds.

Explain to your child that tornadoes are also called "twisters" because they move around and around. Have him/her cut on the lines of the circular pattern to create a "twister."

Let your child try the safety directions below to avoid getting hurt in a tornado.

1. Quickly move close to an inside wall away from windows.

2. Sit facing the wall with your feet under you. Bend over to hide your face.

3. Cover the back of your head with your hands.

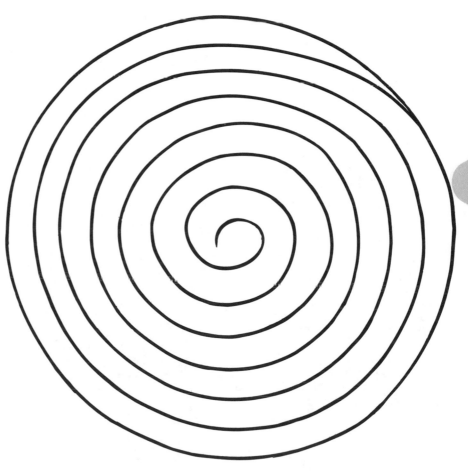

Have your child name safety rules for other types of weather.

This page intentionally left blank.

Snowy Scenes

MR. and MRS. SNOWMAN

Directions: Let your child design a winter picture using crayons or paints on dark construction paper. After he/she is finished, your child can create several snowflakes by using a hole punch and white paper. He/she can glue the snowflakes all over the paper. Tiny pieces of laminating plastic also make interesting snowflakes!

A "Popped" Snowman

Directions: Instruct your child to use white construction paper and scraps of other colors to design a snowman. He/she should glue these on an 8½" x 11" sheet of blue paper. Then, have your child glue popped popcorn all over the snowman's body to create a "snowy" effect. It's fun . . . and yummy!

This page intentionally left blank.

Name_____

Lacy Patterns

Kim likes to look at the lacy patterns of snowflakes with her magnifying glass. Most of them have six sides or six points. But she has never seen two snowflakes that are alike. Kim catches them on small pieces of dark paper so that she can see them better. Some of the snowflakes are broken because they bump into each other as they fall from the clouds.

Color: What does Kim use to make the snowflakes look bigger?

Check: Most snowflakes have ☐ seven ☐ six ☐ five sides or points.

Kim looks at them on dark pieces of paper so that she can . . .

☐ take them to school.   ☐ make a picture.   ☐ see them better.

Write: Why are some of the snowflakes broken?

_____

_____

_____

_____

Name_____

Spring

It is warm in the spring.
Flowers begin to bloom.
Trees have new leaves.
Birds make their nests and lay eggs.
Do you like to fly a kite in the spring?

Directions:

Complete the activities below.

warm   last
_____
- -

Write: It is _____ in the spring.

Circle: What can you see in the spring?

Check: What do birds do in the spring?

☐ Birds make nests.

☐ They lay eggs.

☐ They wash dishes.

Name_____

Summer

Summer can be very hot. It is the time when kids are out of school. They have fun playing with friends, swimming to keep cool and sometimes going on family picnics and vacations.

Directions:

Complete the activities below.

purple   hot

_____

Write: Summer can be very _____

Check: What happens in the summer?

☐ Kids are out of school.

☐ Skunks go on picnics.

☐ Kids play with friends.

Write: What do you like to do in the summer?

_____

Name_____

Autumn

The air gets cool in the autumn.
Kids go back to school. Animals store
food for the winter. Leaves turn red,
yellow and orange. It is a pretty time
of the year.

Directions:

Complete the activities below.

time   cool
_____

Write: The air gets _____ in the autumn.

Check: What happens in the autumn?

☐   Kids go back to school.

☐   Animals store food.

☐   The air is very hot.

Color:

red   yellow   orange

276

Name_____

Winter

Winter can be cold and snowy. Animals stay near each other to stay warm. People wear coats, hats and gloves. Kids make snowmen. It is fun to play in the snow.

Directions:

Complete the activities below.

Check: Winter can be:

☐ cold.

☐ snowy.

☐ purple.

Write:

like   warm

We try to stay _____.

Circle: What do people wear in the winter?

gloves   hat   pan   coat

Name_____

The Four Seasons

1. Write the season words from the Word Bank under the correct boxes below.
2. Color the clothes for autumn **blue**.
3. Color the clothes for winter **red**.
4. Color the clothes for spring green.
5. Color the clothes for summer yellow.

Word Bank	
Spring	Summer
Autumn	Winter

_____

_____

_____

_____

Section 9
Sound

Plastic Cup Telephone

Background Information for the Parent:

Sound is produced by vibrations. This activity illustrates how sound travels. When your child talks into the plastic cup telephone he/she has built, the molecules of air in the cup vibrate. These trapped vibrations make the bottom of the cup vibrate. Tight fishing line carries the vibrations to the other cup bottom, which vibrates and makes the air molecules in that cup vibrate. The listener's eardrums pick up the vibrations, which the brain translates into sound.

A real telephone works along the same principles, but it can reproduce these vibrations with far greater sensitivity, in part because the diaphragms (vibrating disks) for trapping these vibrations are extremely sensitive. (The diaphragm part of the plastic cup telephone is the bottom of the cup.)

Your child should learn from this exercise that his/her vocal cords produce sound by vibrating, that the vibrations are trapped in the cup and that these vibrations are carried along the tight line to the other cup and onto the listener's eardrum.

Activity Suggestions for the Parent:

The fishing line can be any strength, but 10-pound test or above is easier to see and to tie, and it tangles less. You may want to use a short segment of 10 or 15 feet for the first telephone because of its manageable length. A second or third telephone could use lengths of 20 or 30 feet.

With a pencil, have your child poke one hole in the bottom of two plastic cups. Thread the fishing line through the hole in the cup from the bottom side. Tie the line to a paper clip inside the cup and pull on the fishing line to make sure that the line cannot slip out of the cup again. (See illustration on next page.) The paper clip keeps the line from coming out. Follow the same procedures with the other cup.

Explain to your child how the telephone works and that the line must be tight for the phone to carry the sound. You may also need to explain that only one person may talk on the "phone" at a time. The other person has to listen. The phone works best when the person speaks directly into the cup with the cup against the mouth. The listener will hear better if the receiving cup is placed over the ear, blocking out all other sounds.

You can expand this activity by having your child use larger cups, different-shaped cups, different fishing line or varying lengths of fishing line and compare his/her results with the original project.

Activity Sheet: Plastic Cup Telephone

Make a plastic cup telephone!

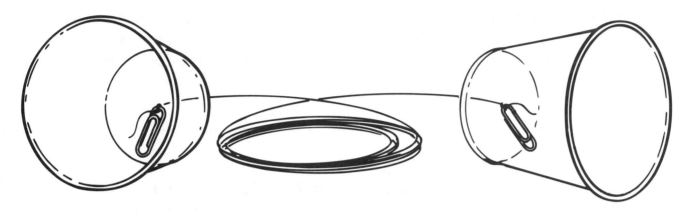

You will need:
fishing line, plastic cups, paper clips, pencil

Directions:

1. Cut a piece of fishing line about 10 feet long.
2. Use a pencil to make a hole in the bottom of each plastic cup.
3. Thread one end of the fishing line through the bottom hole of one cup then tie it to a paper clip.
4. Thread the other end of the fishing line through the bottom hole of the other cup and tie it to a paper clip.

Using the Telephone

1. You and a partner each take a cup.
   Walk apart until the line is tight.
2. One person talks into the cup. The other person listens.

Try This

Make your fishing line longer.

Can you still hear?_____

Milk Carton Banjo

Background Information for the Parent:

Sound is created by vibrations. The frequency of the vibrations determines the pitch. The fewer the vibrations, the lower the pitch. More vibrations create a higher pitch. In a musical instrument or anything else that produces sound, a long string or wire will vibrate fewer times and produce a lower pitch. A short string will vibrate more times and produce a higher pitch.

Activity Suggestions for the Parent:

Milk cartons are ideal for this project because they are sturdy and smooth. The rubber band needs to be long enough to easily wrap around the milk carton from top to bottom. Long, thick, red rubber bands sold in toy stores, craft shops and stationery stores will work well for this activity.

To create a triangular bridge, have your child fold a 4" square piece of cardboard in half and then half again lengthwise. Use a piece of tape to keep the shape. Slide the bridge under the rubber band near the bottom of the milk carton. (See the picture on the next page.) When the banjo is complete, have your child pluck the rubber band above the bridge. Then, he/she should move the bridge an inch toward the top of the carton. This shortens the length of the band. Have your child pluck the rubber band again. The pitch should be a little higher. Have your child move the bridge another inch, shortening the rubber band still more. When he/she plucks the rubber band this time, the pitch will be even higher. Keep moving the bridge and plucking the rubber band until he/she reaches the end of the box. Then, have him/her slide the bridge the other way, and do the same thing.

Your child should grasp the key concept that the shorter rubber band creates a higher pitch. Encourage your child to predict what would happen if he/she used longer boxes, shorter or tighter rubber bands, thicker rubber bands or other variations. Allow your child to experiment with these predictions. This will allow your child to discover that thicker rubber bands vibrate more slowly, and thus have a deeper tone than thinner rubber bands of the same length. Your child will probably recognize that this principle is applied in the guitar and other string instruments to achieve varying pitches.

Activity Sheet: Milk Carton Banjo

This is a milk carton banjo.

You will need:
a half-gallon cardboard milk
carton (or shoe box), cardboard,
a large rubber band, scissors,
tape

Directions:

1. Tape the top of the box closed.
2. Wrap the rubber band around
   the long side of the box and center it.
3. Fold the cardboard in half, and then in
   half again. Make a triangle with the
   cardboard. Tape the cardboard so it stays in
   a triangle. This triangle is called a "bridge."
4. Place the bridge under the rubber
   band near the bottom of the box. Lay the
   back side down on a flat surface.

Playing the Banjo

Pluck the rubber band above the bridge and listen to the sound.

Move the bridge toward the top an inch and pluck the band again.

What happens to the sound? _____

Keep moving the bridge up and plucking the rubber band.

What happens to the sound? _____

Go the other way with the bridge.

What happens to the sound this time? _____

Rubber Band Guitar

Background Information for the Parent:

This activity builds on and reinforces concepts introduced in the previous activities on sound. Vibrations create sound, and the number or frequency of the vibrations determines the pitch. Pitch can be affected by the length and thickness of the object being vibrated.

The lower pitches are produced by longer strings which have slower and fewer vibrations. The higher pitches are produced by shorter strings which have more vibrations which are also faster.

Activity Suggestions for the Parent:

You will want to have your child use the same box and bridge used in the previous activity. Your child will need 4 or 5 long rubber bands. The rubber bands should be all of the same thickness and length for the first part of the experiment. Instruct your child to wrap the rubber bands around the length of the milk carton (or you may use a shoe box). Spread the rubber bands about ¾ inch apart. Slide the bridge under the rubber bands near the top of the carton (or box).

Instruct your child to strum the "guitar" and listen to the sound. Then, have him/her move the bridge forward and strum the guitar again. He/she should note the higher pitch.

Instruct your child to keep moving the bridge and strumming the guitar until the bridge is at the top of the guitar. He/she will note the increasingly higher pitch as the bands are shortened.

After your child has noticed that decreasing the length of the rubber band raises the pitch, instruct him/her to return the bridge to the other end of the guitar.

Place his/her fingers along the rubber bands at various places as shown on the activity sheet. Then, have him/her pluck each string and note how the sounds differ. Next, try different finger arrangements and continue plucking the strings. Your child might also note the various tones achieved by strumming the guitar with these different finger arrangements.

Review the main concepts of vibrations and frequency with your child. Then, ask him/her to demonstrate various fingering arrangements used or to play particularly pleasant tones he/she found while experimenting with the guitar.

You may wish to expand this activity by using different thicknesses of rubber bands for the guitar, with a gradation from very thick at one side to a very thin rubber band at the other side. These rubber bands will introduce the additional concept that thicker strings vibrate more slowly than thinner, lighter ones and produce lower tones at the same length. Allow your child to fully explore the variations created by this instrument.

Name_____

Activity Sheet: Rubber Band Guitar

You will need:
a half-gallon cardboard milk
carton, 4 large rubber bands,
cardboard, tape, scissors

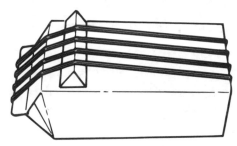

Directions:

1. Tape the top of the box closed.
2. Wrap four rubber bands around the length of the box.
3. Fold the tagboard in half and then in half again.
   Make a triangle with the tagboard. Tape the cardboard
   so it stays in the shape of a triangle. You have made a "bridge."
4. Place the bridge under the rubber bands with the
   flat side down.

Playing the Guitar

Place the bridge at one end
of the box.

Strum the rubber bands.

Move the bridge forward.

Strum again.

What happened to the sound?

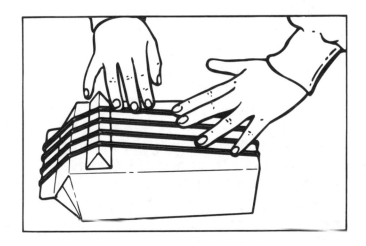

_____

Move the bridge forward again.

How did the sound change?_____

Move the bridge back to the other end.

Place your fingers on the rubber bands at different places.

Pluck each band.

How are the sounds different?_____

If the rubber band is short, will the sound be high or low? _____

Stethoscope

Background Information for the Parent:

Sound can be magnified by using a funnel-shaped tool that gathers and directs them toward the ear. The funnel catches sounds and rushes them to the ear, much as it directs a liquid toward an opening in a bottle. In fact, the ear itself is already shaped to "catch sounds."

The simple stethoscope your child will make uses a funnel to gather the sounds of the heart beating. The tubing is filled with molecules of air which vibrate, and the sound is carried along to the second funnel held at a partner's ear. This funnel magnifies these sounds so that they sound quite clear to the listener.

Activity Suggestions for the Parent:

Tubing for the stethoscope can be any diameter, but $\frac{3}{8}$" or $\frac{1}{2}$" rubber or plastic tubing is ideal. Each stethoscope will use 2–3 feet of tubing. The funnels should have openings no larger than $2\frac{1}{2}$ inches in diameter. Tubing and funnels can be purchased at building supply stores, pet stores and hardware stores.

The stethoscope assembly is shown on the next page. The ends of the funnels should be fitted tightly into the ends of the tubing. Demonstrate the use of the stethoscope and explain that doctors use a very sensitive stethoscope to listen to their patients' hearts and lungs.

Instruct your child to listen while you tap on the other funnel. Take turns listening and tapping until your child is familiar with louder and softer taps.

After he/she is familiar with the stethoscope, have your child listen while you place the second funnel directly over your heart. Demonstrate the exact location of the heart, noting the slightly off-center-to-the-left positioning. Have your child count the number of beats in a minute. The average child's heart beats between 90 and 100 times per minute, although there are individual variations. An adult's heart beats more slowly, about 70 to 80 beats per minute. The heart beats more than 100,000 times each day.

Your child should also position the stethoscope over the lungs and listen for sounds of breathing. He/she should count the number of breaths taken in a minute and then describe the sounds.

You can also listen to a watch tick, measure the heartbeat of a dog or use different substances to tap the funnels, such as erasers, pencils or paper clips. This is also a good time to stress with your child the importance of protecting his/her ears from excessively loud sounds.

Activity Sheet: Stethoscope

You will need:
2 funnels, rubber tubing, watch with a second hand

Directions:

Fit the end of one funnel into one end of the tubing.
Fit the other funnel into the other end of the tubing.
Your stethoscope should look like the one shown here.

Using the Stethoscope

Place one end of the stethoscope over your ear.

Place the other end over your partner's heart.

Listen carefully.

Did you hear the heartbeat?_____

Count the heartbeats in one minute. _____

Now, let your partner count your heartbeats.

How many times did your heart beat in one minute?_____

Lungs

Place the stethoscope over your partner's lungs.

Describe the sounds you heard.

_____

_____

_____

Section 10
Air

Pinwheels

Background Information for the Parent:

A pinwheel demonstrates several scientific principles about air. Moving pinwheels demonstrate that air is a thing and that it occupies space. The resistance of air to objects traveling through it will be seen when your child runs with the pinwheel. The still air pushes against the light paper, and the paper moves. Moving currents of air or wind will move the pinwheel as they push against the paper.

Activity Suggestions for the Parent:

Review the activity sheet instructions with your child. Provide straight pins, a straw, scissors and clear tape.

Demonstrate how far to cut into the pattern (only as far as each line goes) and show your child how to fold each tip down at the center. Tip A goes on top of O, and Tip B goes on top of Tip A. Tip C goes on top of Tip B, and Tip D rests on top of Tip C. Tack these down with a bit of clear tape and run a straight pin through these four tips and the center. Pir. the wheel to a straw and place a bit of tape over the end of the pin and straw so the point is not sticking out. The tape also helps keep the pin in place in the straw.

Your child can use the pinwheel inside or outside, but he/she will get more varied effects outdoors. If the wind is blowing, the air will move the pinwheel. If it is still, your child can run, and the air resistance will twirl the blades. Your child can create his/her own air currents by blowing on the pinwheel.

Your child can create his/her own designs for another pinwheel using different materials, such as construction paper and different sizes and shapes of wheels.

This page intentionally left blank.

Activity Sheet: Pinwheels

Directions:

1. Color the pinwheel.
2. Cut out the pinwheel pattern.
3. Cut along the four diagonal lines.
4. Fold Tip **A** over the center at **O**.
5. Fold Tip **B** over Tip **A** at the center.
6. Fold Tip **C** over Tip **B** at the center.
7. Fold Tip **D** over Tip **C** at the center.
8. Tape these tips in place.
9. Stick a straight pin through the pinwheel and one end of a straw.
10. Tape over the end of the straight pin and the straw.

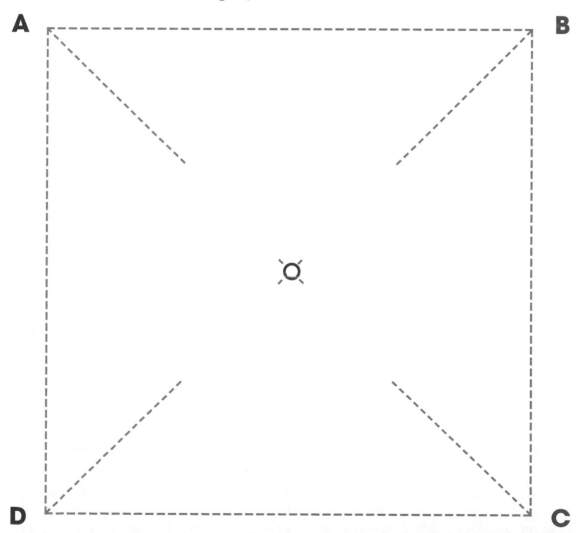

This page intentionally left blank.

Helicopter

Background Information for the Parent:

In a real helicopter, the rotors, or blades, serve both as propellers and as wings. How they are used depends upon how they are tilted. In this model helicopter, the rotors twirl as the helicopter is pulled to the ground. Air occupies the space between the model helicopter and the ground. The molecules of air are very fluid because air is a gas and has no definite shape. The molecules of air provide resistance as the helicopter travels downward. Air gets trapped under the blades of each rotor. This air pushes each rotor blade in a different direction, creating the twirling effect. If the blades were folded in the same direction, the helicopter rotors would not twirl and the model would descend much faster, as there would be less resistance. The speed with which the rotors twirl and the model travels toward the ground is also determined by the amount of weight below the rotors. A small paper clip over the folds increases the speed of descent and the number of twirls the rotors make on their way down. A large paper clip accelerates the movement even more. The width of the rotor blades and the materials they are made from also affect the speed of descent.

Activity Suggestions for the Parent:

Instruct your child to cut out the 2" x 8" pattern from page 295. Next, have him/her cut along the 4" solid line from point A to point B, and then fold Rotor One forward along the dotted line. He/she should next fold Rotor Two backward along the dotted line. Fold section C over section D, D over E and E over F. He/she can then paper clip the fold as shown on the student activity sheet. The helicopter is now ready to fly.

Have your child hold the helicopter by the top of the rotors and let go. The helicopter will twirl to the ground. Your child may want to try dropping the model from higher places, such as from a chair or ladder. You may also have a second-floor balcony or an elevated staircase he/she can use.

Encourage your child's creativity and imagination in creating other versions of the helicopter. Encourage your child to try different materials, sizes and shapes, more rotors, heavier loads and every other variable possible. Some models may be as small as a finger. Some may have four rotors. Some may carry four or five paper clips.

This page intentionally left blank.

Activity Sheet: Helicopter

Directions:

1. Cut out the helicopter pattern.

2. Color the helicopter.

3. Cut along the straight line from point **A** to point **B**.

4. Fold Rotor One forward along the dotted line.

5. Fold Rotor Two backward along the dotted line.

6. Fold sections **C** over **D**, **D** over **E** and **E** over **F** along the dotted lines.

7. Paper clip this fold.

8. Drop the helicopter and observe.

Helicopter Pattern

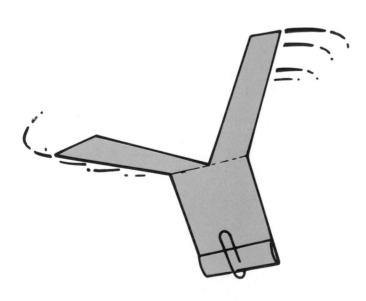

A

Rotor One

Rotor Two

(cut along here)

(fold forward)

(fold backward)

B

(fold on dotted lines)

F

E

D

C

This page intentionally left blank.

Paper Glider

Background Information for the Parent:

A glider is an airplane without a motor. The paper glider your child will make provides an introductory demonstration of the basic forces involved in flight. Even though the paper glider is heavier than air, it can fly for short distances. Gliders are particularly adept at riding currents of air.

Gravity exerts a force on all objects on Earth. This force tends to pull a flying object toward the ground. Lift tends to pull a plane upwards because of lower air pressure on the top of the wing. Thrust is the power used to get a glider airborne—in this case, a quick snap of the wrist. Drag is the resistance of air to objects moving through it. You can feel the drag when you snap your wrists and send the glider off. You sense the resistance of the air.

Activity Suggestions for the Parent:

The basic pattern of the glider is symmetrical. One corner (point A) is folded over to the other side of the paper (point B), and the edges of the paper are lined up. The opposite corner (point C) is then overlapped to the other side (point D). In step 3, the triangular center (point E) is folded back about two inches (point F). The two sides (G and H) are then overlapped.

The fuselage of the glider is created by using a ruler to make a fold on each side, 1 inch (the ruler's width) from the center crease. The edges of each wing are then folded up 1 inch to make the rudders. The ruler is used here also to make the creases sharp.

The glider should be held by the fuselage, using thumb and forefinger, and is sent airborne with a snap of the wrist. This glider works better inside because of its light weight. Your child may develop other places to hold the glider and other techniques for launching it.

Encourage your child to modify the glider's design. The possible variations are many. This extension encourages creativity and applies problem-solving skills in an effective hands-on format which is the richest benefit gained from the lesson. Your child will also find that by turning down one or both rudders, adding paper clips to the nose, cutting elevators on the rear of the glider and so forth, this model will fly a variety of loops, curves and other flight patterns. Every minor modification is, in a sense, a separate mini-investigation.

Activity Sheet:
Paper Glider

You will need: a piece of paper, a ruler

Directions:

1. Fold point **A** over point **B** and line up the edges.
2. Fold point **C** over to point **D**.
3. Fold point **E** back to point **F**.
4. Fold side **G** over side **H**.
5. Use a ruler to fold each side 1 inch from the crease.
6. Use a ruler to fold each rudder up 1 inch from each edge.
7. Launch your glider into flight.

3.

4.

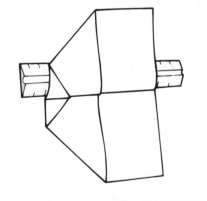

5.

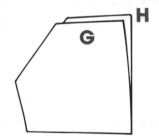

1.

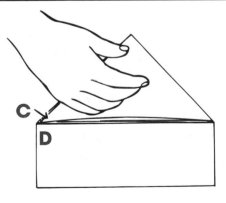

2.

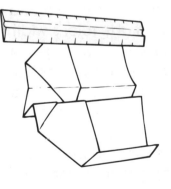

6.

Parachute

Background Information for the Parent:

A parachute is designed to take advantage of the property of air which resists the movement of an object through it. The billowing shape of the parachute traps the moving molecules of air which occupy the atmosphere. The trapped air itself and the resistance to being moved act as a brake on the fall of an object being pulled to the ground by the force of gravity.

The main parts of a parachute are the canopy, the suspension lines and the risers. The canopy is the umbrella-like hood of the chute which traps the air. The suspension lines attach the chute to the person or object falling through the air. Risers are used to control the direction of descent by spilling air out of the chute. (The model does not have risers.)

This project reinforces concepts about the properties of air learned in previous lessons. Among these are that air is a gas, that molecules move very easily, that air is made up of matter and that air occupies space.

Activity Suggestions for the Parent:

Use either a hole punch or scissors to make the holes in the chute for the suspension lines. Stress the need to fold all four dotted lines. Make sure your child understands that the four pieces of fishing line should all be of the same length. You may want your child to use a toy soldier or to create his/her own parachutist from bits of cardboard, wood or other materials.

Your child will want to get as high as possible to drop the parachute. A second-floor staircase, an enclosed balcony or a similar height are ideal. The chute works best if held by the center top when it is dropped.

After this simple model has been used a few times, encourage your child to create new parachutes of different designs. He/she may use different sizes of paper, different materials such as construction paper or cloth, more suspension lines, more folds or none at all or other modifications of his/her own.

This page intentionally left blank.

Activity Sheet: Parachute

Directions:

1. Color the parachute.
2. Cut out the parachute pattern along the outside.
3. Fold the parachute along the dotted lines.
4. Punch or cut a hole in each of the four corners.
5. Tie a 5-inch piece of fishing line to each hole.
6. Tie the four fishing line ends to a toy soldier or some other object.

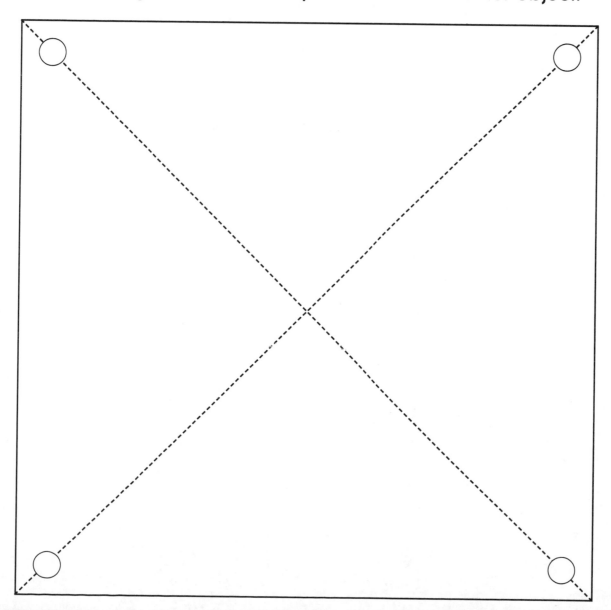

This page intentionally left blank.

Airplane Design

Background Information for the Parent:

Planes and gliders must be designed to accomodate four main forces in flight: weight, lift, thrust and drag.

Weight, or gravity, is the force pulling the plane down. Lift is the opposite force, and it occurs when the air pressure on the top of a wing is less than that underneath the wing. In real airplanes, this lift is induced by using a curved wing. The air travels faster over the top of a curved wing than across the flat underwing. This reduces air pressure on top of the wing and increases it underneath. Thrust is the power that gets a plane into the air and keeps it going. Drag is the air resistance to the plane as it thrusts into and through the air. In this design, the thrust is provided by the person's hand and arm as he/she throws the airplane model into the air. The person doing the throwing can feel the drag as his/her arm whips through the air.

The wings take advantage of the currents of moving molecules and the pressure of the air itself. The plane will fly until the force of gravity overcomes the combined effects of thrust and lift.

Activity Suggestions for the Parent:

This design is a pattern for making the wings, rudder and shaft. The materials used for these parts must be both stiff and flexible. Tagboard, poster board and the material used in file folders all work well. Construction paper is not strong enough.

Your child should lay the patterns on the tagboard and cut out the pieces. He/she should then fold the tagboard with a ruler, using the pattern as a guide. Stress the importance of making straight lines and show him/her how to score the fold lines to make sharp, neat creases. Use rubber cement to glue the parts together. Putting adhesive on both parts to be attached makes a stronger bond. If rubber cement is not available, wood glue, purchased at paint stores or building supply stores, is also very strong. If you need to use regular glue, it is wise to use clear tape along the fold for greater strength and durability.

Your child should check over his/her plane to make sure it resembles the picture, and then allow the glue to dry.

The plane needs weight on the nose of the fuselage before it will fly correctly. Four or five large paper clips are usually sufficient. To fly the plane, have your child hold it between his/her thumb and forefinger directly behind the front wing. He/she should snap the arm and wrist forward and slightly up. The plane should glide freely through the air quite well. If the plane turns sharply up, it needs more weight on the nose. If it falls too soon, it has too much weight or your child did not let go in time when he/she launched the plane. This plane is best flown outside because of its size and weight. If it is windy, launch the plane into the wind, being careful to fly the plane away from obstructions and other people.

By the end of this activity, your child should be quite comfortable with the basic vocabulary of the airplane and aware of the basic forces which affect flight.

This page intentionally left blank.

Name_____

Activity Sheet:
Airplane Design/Part I

You will need:

tagboard, glue (or tape), scissors, ruler

Directions:

1. Cut out the shaft pattern on this sheet.
2. Glue this pattern on a piece of tagboard.
3. Trim off the extra tagboard.
4. Use a ruler to fold the tagboard shaft along the pattern lines.
5. Score each fold with scissors.
6. Overlap two sides of the shaft to form a triangle.
7. Glue or tape the shaft in this shape.

This is what your plane will look like when you are done.

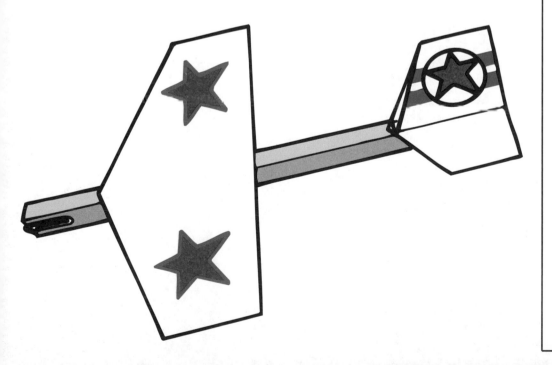

This page intentionally left blank.

Activity Sheet: Airplane Design/Part II

Directions:

1. Cut out the front wing pattern.
   Use this pattern to cut a wing from tagboard.

2. Cut out the rear wing pattern.
   Use this pattern to cut a wing from tagboard.

Wing Patterns

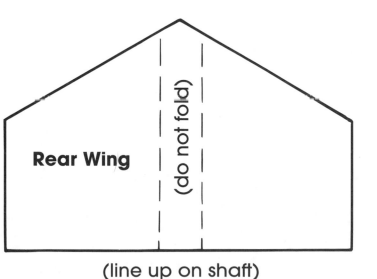

(use dotted line to
line up wing on shaft)

Front Wing

(do not fold)

Rear Wing

(do not fold)

(line up on shaft)

This page intentionally left blank.

Activity Sheet:
Airplane Design/Part III

Directions:

Cut out the rudder pattern. Use this pattern to cut a rudder from tagboard.

Rudder Pattern

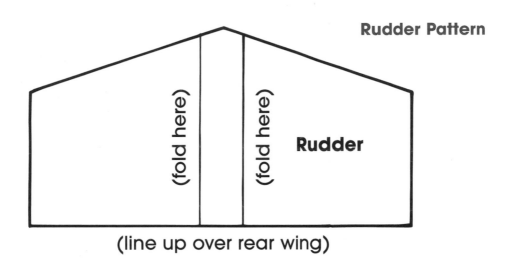

(fold here) (fold here) **Rudder**

(line up over rear wing)

Putting It All Together

1. Line up the front wing on the shaft $1\frac{1}{2}$ to 2 inches from the nose. Glue it on.
2. Line up the rear wing at the end of the shaft. Glue it on.
3. Line up the rudder on top of the rear wing. Glue it on. Glue the tips together. Place 4 to 6 large paper clips on the nose of the plane. Tape them on.
4. Fly your airplane!

This page intentionally left blank.

Name_____

The Dancing Coin

Can you make a coin dance on the top of a bottle? Let's try!

You will need:

a glass soft-drink bottle
a coin

1. Wet the rim of an empty bottle and one side of the coin.

2. Place the wet side of the coin on the rim of the bottle.

3. Hold the bottle with your warm hands. Watch closely!

What happened?
Your warm hands heated the cool air inside the bottle. The air expanded and tried to escape. It pushed on the coin and made it "dance!"

Name_____

The Crusher

Can you crush a plastic soft-drink bottle without even touching it? Let's try it!

You will need:

a plastic soft-drink bottle and cap
hot water
cold water

1. Fill the bottle with hot water from the faucet. Let the bottle stand for a minute.

2. Pour out the hot water. Quickly screw on the cap. Make sure the cap is on tightly.

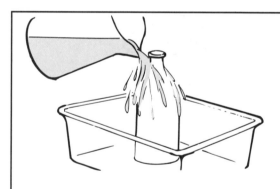

3. Pour a pitcher of very cold water over the bottle or hold the bottle under the cold water faucet. Watch what happens!

What happened?
The hot water made the air in the bottle very warm. The bottle cap captured the warm air in the bottle. The cold water made the warm air become cold. Cold air takes less space, and the air pressure outside the bottle pushed in the sides of the bottle.

Name_____

Powerful Push-Up

Can air hold up water? It can, with a little help
from you! Let's find out how!

You will need:

a drinking glass
a card the size of a postcard
water

1. Fill the glass to overflowing.

2. Lay the card on top of the glass.

3. Hold the card down with one
hand. Turn the glass over. Remove
your hand. What happened?

What happened?
Air pushes in all directions. The air pressure pushing up under the card
is greater than the pressure of the water pushing down. The card stays
in place.

High and Dry

Can you put a piece of paper under water without getting it wet? You can do it with a little help from air pressure. Let's try!

You will need:

a drinking glass
a sheet of paper
a sink full of water

1. Crumple a sheet of paper. Push it into the bottom of the glass so that it stays in place.

2. Hold the glass upside down.

3. Push it straight down into the water.

What happened?
The glass is full of air. The water cannot enter the glass because the air inside the glass exerts pressure on the water. If you tilt the glass, however, the air escapes and water enters.

Simple Machines

Name_____

Lifting with Levers

A lever is a simple machine used to lift or move things.
It has two parts. The **arm** is the part that moves.
The **fulcrum supports** the arm, but does not move.

Label the parts of this lever. _____

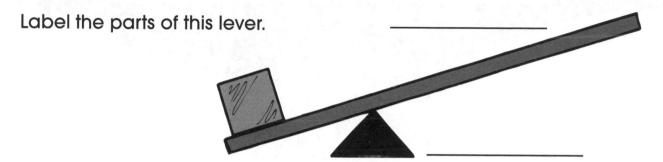

_____

Unscramble the names of these kinds of levers.

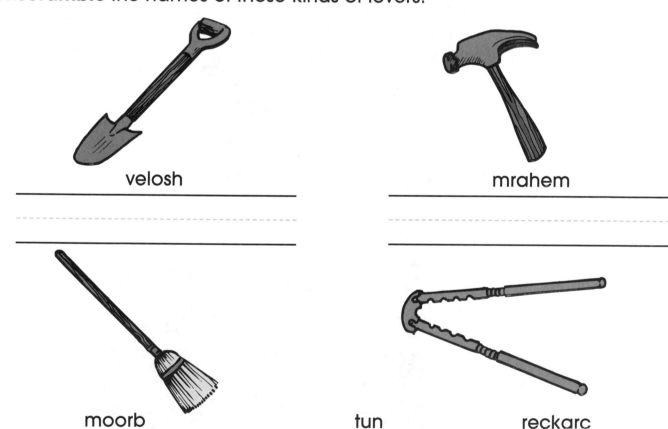

velosh
_____
_____

mrahem
_____
_____

moorb
_____
_____

tun   reckarc
_____
_____

Name_____

Levers at Work

Levers help make our work easier. Color all the levers.
Then, find their names in the word search.

```
c a n o p e n e r d
r s d d l j k l m n
o h s c i s s o r s
w v h b e z x c a a
b t o b r z o a k r
a d v n s u k f s m
r u e h a m m e r g
w f l h g f a d s v
```

Name_____

Machine with a Slant

An **inclined plane** has a slanted surface. It is used to move things from a low place to a high place. Some inclined planes are smooth. Others have steps.

Directions: Color the inclined planes in the picture.

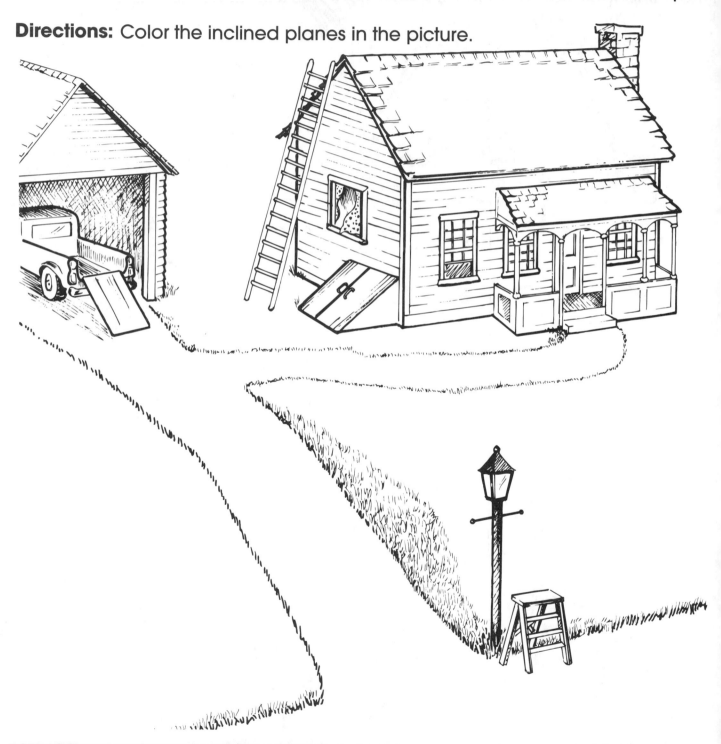

The Wedge

A **wedge** is a type of inclined plane. It is made up of two inclined planes joined together to make a sharp edge. A wedge can be used to cut things. Some wedges are pointed.

Directions: Color the pictures of wedges.

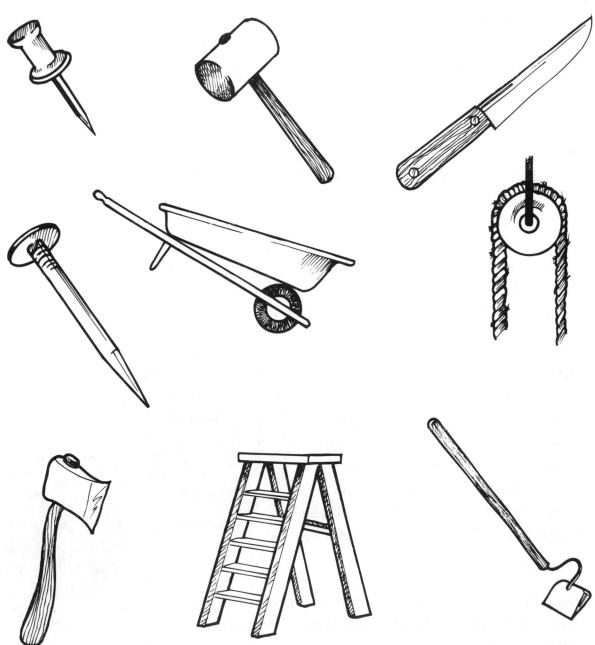

Wheel and Axle

How do wheels work? The two activities below will help your child understand how wheels work and how wheels help to make our work easier!

You will need:

a cardboard box, string, four wooden spools, two pieces of wire or pipe cleaners long enough to serve as axles, staples or brass fasteners to fasten the "axles" to the box, heavy items to add weight to the box

Activity #1:

Have your child tie the string to the box. Put the items in the box, and let your child pull the box. Ask him/her: How hard is it to pull? How can we use the spools to help us? Run each pipe cleaner (axle) through the two spools, and fasten the pipe cleaners to the box with the fasteners so that a little wagon is constructed. Now, let your child try pulling the box again. Ask your child: How does this change the amount of strength it takes to move the wagon?

Activity #2:

Your child will need a heavy book and two pencils. Ask your child to try to move the book along the surface of a table with just one finger. Ask: Is this easy or hard to do? Let him/her now rest the book on the two pencils. Ask your child how the pencil "wheels" affect the amount of effort it takes to move the book.

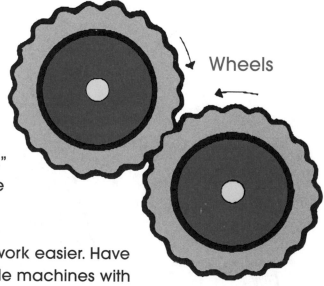

Wheels

Talk with your child about how wheels make work easier. Have your child think of as many examples of simple machines with wheels as he/she can.

Screws

A screw is a very helpful simple machine. It can be used to hold two pieces of wood together. It cannot be pulled easily out of wood like smooth nails.

Directions:

1. Color part of the inclined plane as shown below.

2. Cut out the inclined plane.

3. Wrap it around a pencil as shown.

4. Tape it at the bottom.

5. Twirl the pencil with your fingers. What does it look like?

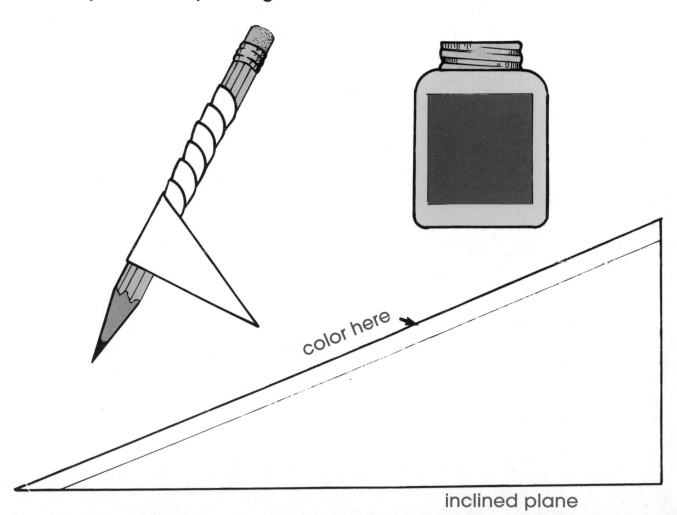

color here

inclined plane

This page intentionally left blank.

Pulleys

Try the first activity with your child to help him/her build an under-standing of how pulleys work. Then, build your own pulley!

You will need:
rope or wire, a pulley, a stick, two tall chairs or other supports for the stick and a bundle of heavy books

Let your child try to lift the bundle of heavy books. Ask your child: Is it easy or hard to lift the books? Now, suspend the stick between the two tall chairs and attach the pulley to the stick. Tie the bundle of books to one end of the rope, and thread the rope through the pulley. Now, let your child try "lifting" the book bundle by pulling down on the free end of the rope. Ask your child to describe the difference in the amount of effort needed.

Make Your Own Pulley!

You will need:
an empty thread spool
a piece of wire

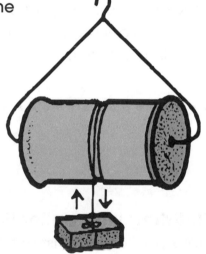

Directions:

1. Using about 10-20 inches of wire, help your child thread the wire through the hole in the spool.

2. Bend the ends of the wire up to hold the spool in place.

3. Twist them together forming a hook by which the spool "pulley" can be suspended from a rod. Make sure the spool spins loosely on the wire. Cutting a slight notch across the center of the spool helps keep the load-carrying string in place.

Let your child have fun experimenting with his/her miniature pulley!

Building with Simple Machines

Building with a Lever
Let your child try lifting a heavy block or rock, with or without a lever. (Use a triangular block as a fulcrum.) Try putting the fulcrum at various locations to see which way is the easiest. Experiment with a seesaw on the playground, or construct a miniature one for dolls in a playhouse.

Building with an Inclined Plane
Help your child construct a simple inclined plane with building blocks and boards. Let him/her try sliding a heavy object up or down the ramp instead of lifting it. Talk about the advantages of using an inclined plane.

Let your child play in a playhouse area and experiment with taking doll carriages or wagons down steps, and then try the same thing with an inclined plane. Ask your child what he/she notices. Talk about how inclined planes make work easier.

Building with Simple Machines

Building with Wheels

Help your child make three simple carts from empty cartons (cigar or shoe boxes) using the instructions from Activity #1 on page 320. Make three sets of wheels from heavy chipboard (or plywood), one set in a square shape, another set in a triangular shape and the last set in a circular shape. Attach the wheels to the carts, using wire or nails to serve as axles. Allow your child to "race" the carts, and he/she will quickly see which set of wheels is the most efficient.

Cut corrugated paper (cardboard) to fit around two large thread spools. Insert a large nail through the spool opening and nail it loosely to a square board, allowing the corrugated paper to mesh as cogs. Let your child manipulate the "wheels" by turning one spool, discovering that one wheel may make another wheel work—just like clocks and other machines!

Building with Screws

Let your child play with nuts and bolts. It is fun for children to match and fit together the various sizes of nuts with the proper bolts.

Drill some small holes in a wooden board. Let your child have fun (and practice fine motor skills!) using a screwdriver and screws. Let your child put the screws in the holes in the wooden board. Ask your child how he/she thinks screws can help to make work easier.

Name_____

The Right Tool for the Job

Mother gave Tyrone and Kim a list of jobs. Help them pick the right tool for each job. Draw a line from the job to the tool.

What will help Kim raise the flag up the flagpole?

inclined plane

What will Tyrone use to help him get the cat out of the tree?

pulley

What will Kim use to carry sand to her new sandbox?

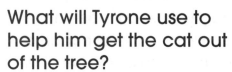

lever

What will Tyrone use to get the nail out of the board?

screw.

What will Kim use to hang the mirror on her bedroom door?

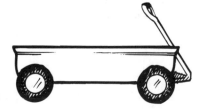

wheel and axle

What will Tyrone use to slice the turkey?

wedge

Name_____

Six Simple Machines

Welcome to Simon's Simple Machine Shop! Simon needs some help putting his simple machines where they belong. Color and cut out each simple machine. Glue each one in the correct place.

Simon's Simple Machine Shop

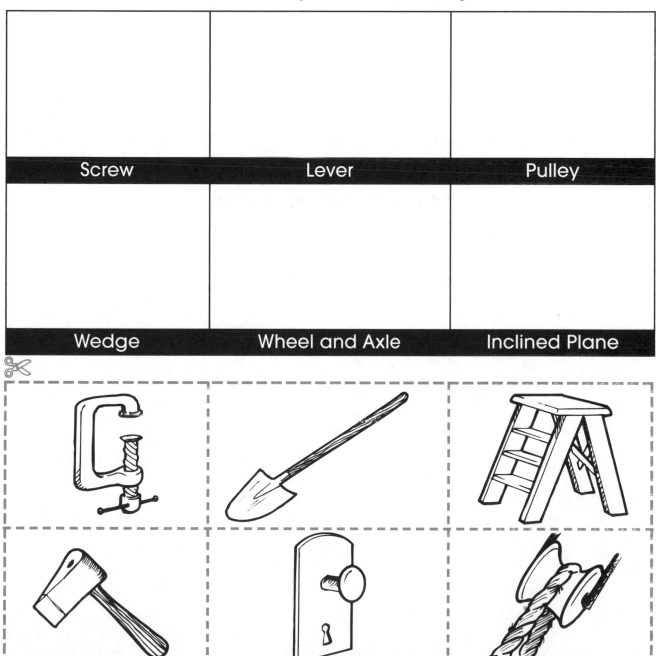

Screw	Lever	Pulley
Wedge	Wheel and Axle	Inclined Plane

This page intentionally left blank.

As Easy as 1 - 2 - 3!

Machines make our work easier. There are many kinds of machines. Some machines are big and some are small. Some machines have many parts while some have just one.

Directions: Color and cut out the machines at the bottom of this page. Glue each one next to the picture that shows where it is needed on the Job Chart below.

Job Chart

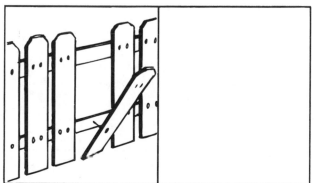

This page intentionally left blank.

Who Am I?

Directions: Use the words in the Word Bank to name the simple machine in each picture. Then, you will find the answer to this question.

What do machines use to do work?

1.

2.

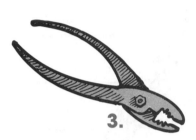

3.

1. ___ ___ ☐ ___ ___ ___ ___ ___ ___ ___ ___ ___

2. ___ ___ ___ ___ ☐ ___ ___ ___ ___ ___ ___ ___

3. ___ ___ ☐ ___ ___ ___

4. ___ ___ ___ ☐ ___ ___ ___

5. ___ ___ ___ ☐ ___ ___

6. ___ ___ ___ ☐ ___ ___ ___

4.

5.

6.

Word Bank		
wheel and axle	inclined plane	screw
wedge	lever	pulley

Name_____

Ready for Work!

Directions: Read the names of the tools in the Word Bank.
Write each tool under the correct kind of simple machine.

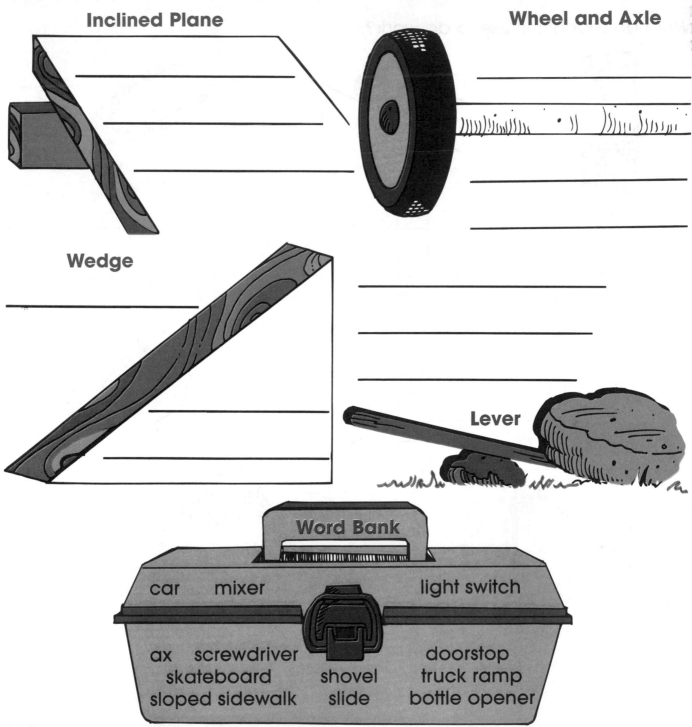

Inclined Plane

_____

_____

_____

Wheel and Axle

_____

_____

_____

Wedge

_____

_____

_____

Lever

_____

_____

_____

Word Bank

car   mixer   light switch

ax   screwdriver   doorstop
skateboard   shovel   truck ramp
sloped sidewalk   slide   bottle opener

Section 12

Magnets

Working with Magnets

Background Information for the Parent:

All magnets are surrounded by a magnetic field which is made up of invisible lines of force. These lines of force can be visually demonstrated by spreading iron filings on a sheet of paper and holding a magnet under the paper. The filings will be drawn in a neat, uniform pattern to the magnet. The patterns can be varied by moving the magnet, using different sides or ends of the magnet and by varying the distance of the magnet from the paper and filings.

Magnets attract certain metals, primarily iron and steel. They are not attracted to aluminum foil, coins or most other metals. Magnets are attracted to each other.

There are many different kinds and types of magnets of widely varying strength. Some of the most common magnets are bar magnets, horseshoe magnets and disk magnets. Large magnets are usually much stronger than smaller magnets, but two magnets of the same size can vary considerably in power.

Activity Suggestions for the Parent:

The magnets for this activity do not need to be large or expensive. Neither do all magnets need to be the same size or type. Many magnets are rubberized and these are often available in economical packages costing a few dollars. Other magnets you might consider are cylindrical cow magnets. Some rectangular and square magnets are sold inexpensively in toy stores and science supply catalogs.

Iron filings can be purchased from catalogs, toy stores, some craft shops and other similar places. Spreading the iron filings on a sheet of construction paper or some other stiff paper will keep them relatively contained.

Your child will notice the ease with which even the smallest magnet will attract the filings. He/she will enjoy trying to make different patterns with a magnet held underneath the paper and filings.

Having your child pick up paper clips with a magnet is a good way to test the relative strength of each magnet he/she uses. He/she can record the number of paper clips picked up. Have him/her gather all the data he/she can by measuring the strength of every available magnet.

Activity Sheet: Working with Magnets

Directions:

Spread some iron filings on a sheet of paper.

Move a magnet near them.

What happened?

_____

Hold a magnet above the filings.

What happened?

_____

Move the magnet around **under** the paper.

What happened?

_____

Draw

On another sheet of paper, draw pictures of some of the patterns you made with the magnet and iron filings.

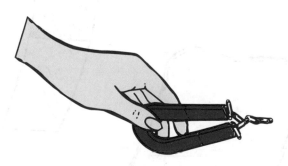

Testing Magnets

Test several magnets.
Tell how many paper clips each magnet picked up.

	Type of Magnet	Number Picked Up
Magnet #1		
Magnet #2		
Magnet #3		

Magnetic Pull

Directions: Draw a line from the magnet to each thing that it can pull.

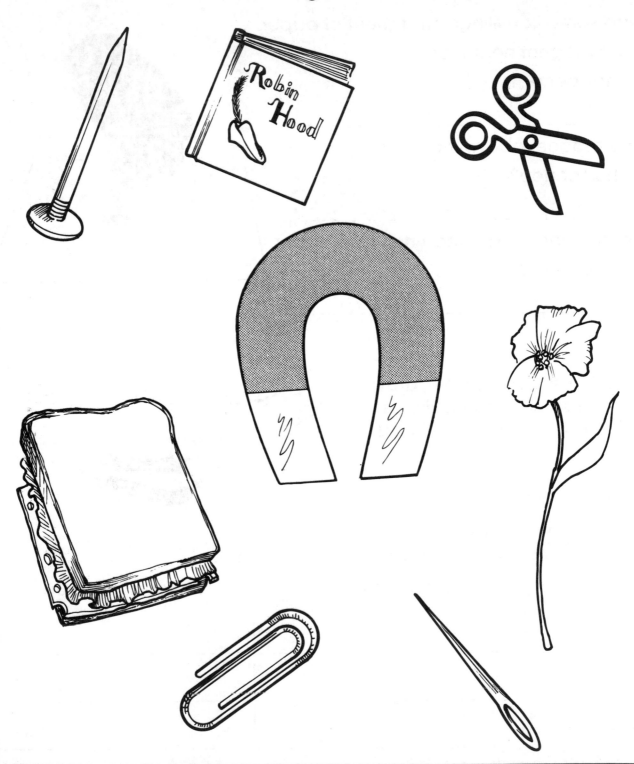

"Attractive" Magnets

Directions: Cut out each object and glue it on the chart where it belongs. Use a crayon to graph the results.

Will Attract	Will Not Attract

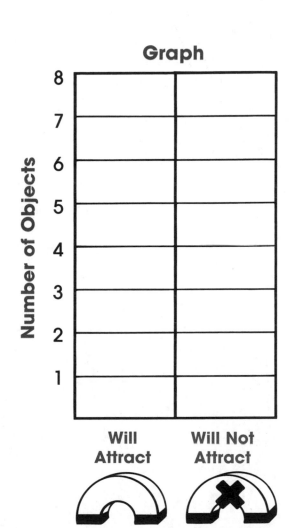

Graph

Number of Objects

8
7
6
5
4
3
2
1

Will Attract   Will Not Attract

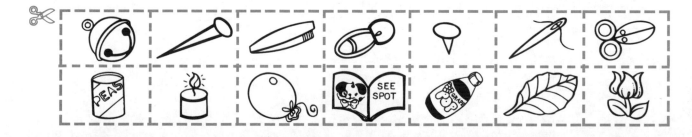

This page intentionally left blank.

Using a Compass

Background Information for the Parent:

Compasses have been used for at least 800 years as instruments for determining directionality while traveling. They may have been in use as long as 4,500 years ago in China. They are based on the simple principles of magnetism. A compass is a free-floating magnet which points to magnetic north.

The Earth operates as a huge magnet with invisible lines of force radiating from the north and south magnetic poles. Magnetic north is about 1,000 miles from true geographic north. Magnetic south is about 1,600 miles from true geographic south. Nonetheless, a compass points in the general direction of north and is very useful because of this. It can, however, give distorted readings if used next to a strong magnet or a lot of iron or steel.

Activity Suggestions for the Parent:

Although this project can be done inside most buildings, it is more dramatic and enjoyable if done outside. Small hand compasses can be purchased from science supply catalogs.

Allow your child to become familiar with the instructions and the compass before you give some guided directions. Your child needs to know which end of the needle faces north. Usually, that end is painted silver, blue or red. Once that is determined, he/she should locate and record a large object as a reference point for north.

After your child has become oriented to finding north, have him/her hold the compass with "N" at the top of the compass. Your child should then turn to the left until he/she is facing west. The needle will still point to the north. Have your child record the name of a significant object in that direction. He/she should then turn left until facing south. (The needle facing north will be pointing directly at the child.) After recording a significant object in the south, one more turn to the left will point them to the east which he/she will remember with some object in that direction.

After this initial orientation, encourage your child to close his/her eyes and turn around to some point and open his/her eyes. Your child should try to find the directions he/she is facing using the compass. You might have him/her turn to the sound of your voice or work with a partner following the partner's directions.

This is also an opportunity to introduce the intermediate directions on the compass: northwest, southwest, southeast and northeast. Your child could also do a follow-up activity locating landmarks in each of these four directions.

Activity Sheet: Using a Compass

This is a compass.
It can tell you what direction you are facing.

N - North

S - South

E - East

W - West

Hold your compass.

Turn your body until you and the compass
are pointing north.

Name one large object you see to the north. _____

Turn to the left until you are facing west.

Name one large object in the west._____

Turn left again until you are facing south.

Name one large object in the south. _____

Turn left again until you are facing east.

Name one large object in the east._____

Try This

Close your eyes.

Turn around.

Look at your compass.

What direction are you facing? _____

Making a Needle Compass

Background Information for the Parent:

A piece of steel, such as a needle, can be magnetized and will remain magnetic for quite a while. To magnetize the needle, a bar magnet is rubbed against the needle between 10 and 40 times, depending on the magnetic strength desired. It is very important that the magnet be rubbed only one way against the needle. Going back and forth will erase the magnetic effect.

Small particles within a needle are each a tiny magnet. Rubbing the needle with the bar magnet lines up these tiny molecular magnets so that the poles all face the same direction. The needle will thus have a north pole and a south pole and be magnetized. Polarity is determined by the end of the needle that is rubbed and by the pole of the magnet that does the rubbing. If your magnet is marked north and south, rub the south pole of the magnet against the sharp point of the needle. The sharp point will then point north.

Activity Suggestions for the Parent:

Regular sewing needles purchased in a grocery store work well for this. So will small paper clips. Just straighten them out and mark one end.

Inexpensive bar magnets can be purchased from science supply catalogs. Some craft stores sell inexpensive rubberized magnets that will also work well. Hardware and building supply stores sell cork in sheets for less than a dollar. Cut the cork into 1-inch square pieces with scissors. Your child will need a plastic cup of water, a 1-inch square of cork, a needle, a small bar magnet and a compass.

Explain to your child that it is very important to rub the magnet only one way, not back and forth. Ideally, he/she should make a wide swing so that the magnet will not erase or neutralize the effects of each rubbing. The needle might be magnetized with as few as 10 strokes, but stroking the needle 40 times each will make certain that it is highly magnetized.

The magnetized needle can be placed on the cork. Use masking tape to hold it securely on the cork. Float the cork on the water in the plastic cup. The needle should point north. Your child can check the accuracy of the needle with a regular compass. Make certain the regular and the homemade compasses are not too close to each other or they will disorient each other. The bar magnet should also be set off to the side.

After this investigation, your child can examine the effect of the bar magnet on the needle by circling the plastic cup's exterior with the bar magnet. The magnet will attract the needle and make it within circle the cup.

Review the concepts with your child when you conclude this investigation. Encourage him/her to extend the activity by trying to magnetize other materials such as nails, pins, large paper clips, darning needles and so forth.

Activity Sheet: Making a Needle Compass

Directions:

1. Rub the needle against the magnet 40 times.
2. Rub only one way.
3. Place the needle on the cork.
4. Attach it with tape.

Using Your Compass

Place the cork in the water.

Which way does the needle point? _____

Did your real compass point the same way? _____

Try This

Hold your magnet next to the plastic cup.

Circle the cup with your magnet.

What does the needle do? _____

Magnet Magic

Background Information for the Parent:
Magnetism is a natural force. Magnets have different sizes, shapes and strengths. Magnetic force can pass through different materials.

Activity:
Explain to your child that magnets have a north pole that always seeks the Earth's magnetic north pole. They also have a south pole that seeks the Earth's magnetic south pole. Let him/her try to bring together two like poles. What do they do? (It feels as though a force is pushing the magnets apart. They "repel" each other.) Then, have your child try to bring a north and a south end together. What happens this time? (The two attract each other.) Have your child record his/her findings.

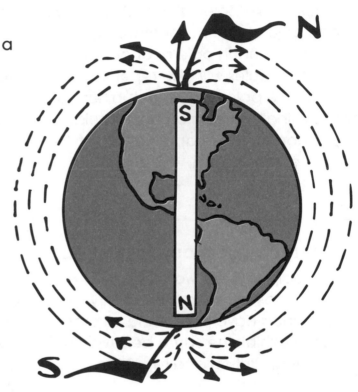

Extension:
Demonstrate that the needle of a compass is a magnet because its north-seeking pole always points north.

Push or Pull?

Background Information for the Parent:

Every magnet, regardless of shape, has a north pole and a south pole. The north pole of one magnet is attracted to the south pole of another magnet and vice versa. Thus, unlike poles attract each other. The north pole of one magnet will repel, or push away, the north pole of another magnet. The south poles will also repel each other. Thus, like poles repel each other. An understanding of attraction and repulsion is very important to the applications of the principles of magnetism.

All magnets have a magnetic field composed of invisible force lines which surround them. This can be demonstrated when a magnet is placed under a paper holding iron filings. The filings are drawn into an arrangement that illustrates these lines of force. Taping two magnets together with their like poles touching and holding this arrangment under the paper will show two lines of iron filings and two lines of force repelling each other.

Activity Suggestions for the Parent:

Large bar magnets would be the easiest ones to use for this activity, but all magnets have poles, and all magnets will exhibit the same behavior in terms of attraction and repulsion.

This activity will require little direction from you, although you will probably want to review some key words before allowing your child to begin. Your child should feel the attraction of the magnets for each other when he/she holds the unlike poles near each other. He/she should notice that the attraction increases when the magnets get closer to each other.

Your child may be even more amazed at the force exhibited when the like poles are held near each other. He/she should be able to feel the resistance as the like poles are forced closer and closer to each other. The resistance is quite dynamic with large bar magnets or hand-sized horseshoe magnets.

Allow some unstructured time for your child to investigate other properties of these magnets and to develop his/her own activities.

Activity Sheet: Push or Pull?

Every magnet has a north pole and a south pole.

When a north pole and a south pole are next to each other, they pull together.

When two north poles, or two south poles, are next to each other, they push apart.

Directions: Tell what each pair of magnets will do below. Write **push** or **pull.**

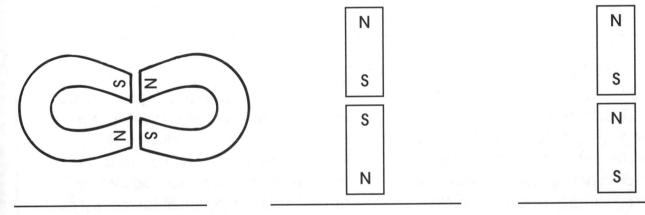

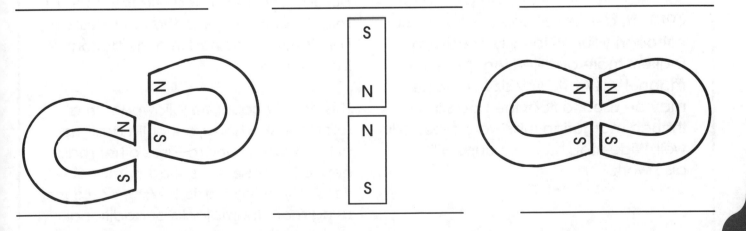

Cork Boats

Background Information for the Parent:

Magnets have invisible lines of force which surround them. This magnetic field will function even through other materials, such as plastic, water, wood and paper. The thickness of the material and the distance of the magnet from the object to be attracted determine if the object will be drawn to the magnet. The strength of the magnet also determines how far away the magnet can be and still attract an object.

In this exercise, the magnet is held near a plastic cup or container. It has to attract the thumbtacks through the plastic, the water and in one part of the investigation, through the cork. A strong magnet will easily attract through these materials. In fact, if the magnet is too strong, it might even sink the boat. If the magnet does not work because it is too weak, have your child try combining two or more magnets. However, usually even a small magnet will work.

Activity Suggestions for the Parent:

Your child will be making cork boats. The cork can easily be obtained at building supply places for less than a dollar a sheet. Cut a piece 1 inch wide and 1 or 2 inches long. Round toothpicks are sturdier and work better for the mast than the thinner flat ones. The sail may be made of a simple triangle cut from a scrap of construction paper, although your child may choose to make it more detailed. Any type of magnet will work. Any size container may be used to float the boats in, though margarine tubs work especially well. Wide-mouth plastic cups will also work.

Scotch tape or masking tape may be used to attach the paper sail to the toothpick mast. The toothpick sticks into the soft cork and stands upright. The four thumbtacks are pushed into the bow, or front, of the boat for the first part of the investigation. Later they are pulled out and pushed into the deck, or middle, of the boat. In the last investigation, they are pushed into the bottom of the boat.

This activity could be followed with a related task where your child designs different boats and/or uses other magnets to increase the speed or maneuverability of the boats. He/she could try using more thumbtacks or additional metal on the boats.

Activity Sheet: Cork Boats

You will need:
cork, a toothpick, 4 thumbtacks, a plastic
margarine tub

Directions:

1. Stick the toothpick into the cork.
2. Tape a sail to the toothpick.
3. Stick four thumbtacks in the front
   of the boat.

Sailing the Boat

Place the boat on the water in your tub.

Hold the magnet against the tub.

Does the boat move?_____

Try This

Stick the thumbtacks in the middle of the boat.
Can you make the magnet move the boat?

_____

Now stick the thumbtacks on the bottom of the boat.
Can you control the boat by moving the magnet
under the tub?

_____

Strong Magnet!

This activity will help your child understand that magnets can exert their force through a variety of materials. Your child will test a magnet's force through a paper plate, a plastic cup, a plastic cup full of water and a thin booklet. Let your child select one of the items listed, and ask: If a magnet is placed on top of this paper plate, will a magnet held underneath the plate be able to move it?

Let your child predict the results for each item, and then test it out for him/herself. Let your child discuss with you what he/she discovered.

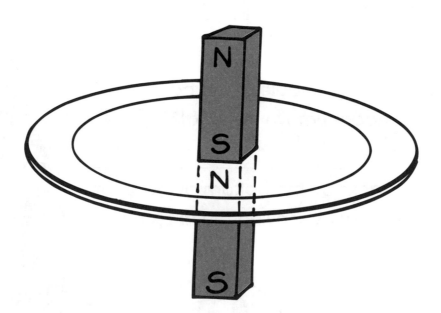

Glossary

A

amphibian: An animal that is cold-blooded, hatches from an egg and has smooth, moist skin. An amphibian lives part of its life in water and part on land.

B

brain stem: The part of the brain that controls your breathing and heartbeat.

buoyancy: The ability of an object to float.

C

calcium: A mineral needed for strong bones.

capillary action: Liquid moving upward through small openings.

cerebellum: The part of the brain which controls the movement of your muscles and makes them move smoothly.

cerebrum: The largest part of the brain. The cerebrum is the part of the brain which does your thinking.

chrysalis: A protective covering for a caterpillar while it changes into a butterfly.

cohesion: Molecules of water clinging together to form a drop.

compass: A free-floating magnet which determines directionality.

condensation: The joining together of water molecules in the air to form droplets.

conserve: To save.

D

digestive system: The organs which break down food (esophagus, stomach, small intestine, large intestine, liver).

displacement: Being removed from the original position.

E

environment: The living and non-living parts of the world around us.

esophagus: The food tube which connects the mouth to the stomach.

evaporation: The process in which water has changed from liquid form to a gas because of the heat of the sun.

F

fossil: An outline of the physical remains of an organism which lived long ago.

fulcrum: The part of a lever which supports the arm and remains stationary.

G

geology: The study of rocks, minerals and Earth's history.

germs: Microscopic organisms that can make you sick.

gravity: A force which pulls toward the center of the Earth and gives things weight.

H

hibernation: A deep sleep during the cold winter months in order to conserve energy and body fat.

I

inclined plane: A slanted surface, a simple machine.

insect: An organism that has three body sections, three pair of legs and a hard outer skeleton called an exoskeleton.

intestine: Part of the digestive system which breaks down food and separates it from waste.

invertebrate: Animal that has no backbone or internal skeleton.

L

lever: A simple machine used to lift or move things.

liver: Part of the digestive system which helps to digest sugars.

M

mammal: Animals that are warm-blooded, breathe air, have live babies and feed their young milk.

magnet: A bar which attracts metals such as iron and steel.

magnify: To make objects appear larger than they actually are.

metamorphosis: A change in the form of an insect.

migration: Traveling to warmer climates to avoid cold weather.

muscles: Organs that make your body move by working together to bend and straighten your joints.

O

oxygen: A gas you breathe.

P

precipitation: Water vapor which condenses and forms droplets which fall to Earth as rain, snow, sleet or hail.

pulley: A rope and wheel used to lift things, a simple machine.

R

recycle: To use something again.

reptile: An animal that has scales, lays eggs and is cold-blooded.

S

sedimentary rocks: Rocks formed by tiny particles such as clay and sand.

skeleton: All of your bones.

stethoscope: Hearing device which allows you to hear a heartbeat.

surface tension: Water molecules pulling together so that a "skin" is created on the surface.

T

thermometer: An instrument which measures temperature.

tornado: Spiraling wind with a funnel-shaped cloud associated with thunderstorms.

V

vertebrate: An animal whose skeleton has a backbone.

W

wedge: Two inclined planes connected to make a sharp edge, a simple machine.